CW01512222

Travellers, Gypsies, Roma:
The Demonisation of Difference

Travellers, Gypsies, Roma:
The Demonisation of Difference

Edited by

Michael Hayes and Thomas Acton

CAMBRIDGE SCHOLARS PUBLISHING

Travellers, Gypsies, Roma: The Demonisation of Difference, edited by Michael Hayes
and Thomas Acton

This book first published 2007 by

Cambridge Scholars Publishing

15 Angerton Gardens, Newcastle, NE5 2JA, UK

British Library Cataloguing in Publication Data
A catalogue record for this book is available from the British Library

TABLE OF CONTENTS

INTRODUCTION

The social history of Travellers and Roma remained largely undocumented up to recent times. In Ireland the Traveller community scores high on all indicators of social disadvantage relating to health, unemployment, education, and infant and adult mortality. Their social history shares many similarities with the Roma (Gypsies) who number at least twelve million people worldwide Roma are referred to by a variety of different names - Gypsies Tsigani, Tzigane, Cigano, Zigeuner, and quite a few more. Like the Irish Travellers they too have suffered a long history of discrimination in terms of employment, education, health care and other services. While the pogroms of the Nazi terror of World War II - the Porrajmos (Holocaust) - with estimates of deaths ranging between 400,000 and 1.5 million Roma - is the most infamous example of anti-Roma prejudice in European history, the collapse of the communist regimes post 1989 have rekindled anti-Roma sentiment in both Eastern and Western Europe. A resurfacing of national and ethnic tensions in the former Eastern Bloc has contributed to increased levels of anti-Roma prejudice and often violent attacks against Romani immigrants and refugees has also acted as a catalyst for some Roma to migrate to West European countries, such as Ireland and the U.K., in search of a better life.

The scholars and activists contributing to this volume have all engaged with such questions as ethnicity, identity, ethnology, linguistics, racism, cultural expression and the new historiography that characterise the disciplines now referred to as Traveller Studies and Romani Studies. Of particular concern to this volume has been the necessity to address these broader issues within the context of the ever-changing dynamics of representation, modernisation, globalisation and the re-construction of the nation-state within the European Union. It is hoped that this volume of essays will function as a catalyst for the disciplines of Irish Studies, Traveller Studies, Romani Studies and Migration Studies.

This volume of essays is an eclectic mix of brief narratives and more academically oriented essays on areas as diverse as: an English Romani perspective on the Surrey Project (Jake Bowers); human rights (Thomas Acton); policing in the U.K. (Colm Power), housing (Joanna Richardson) and anti-trespassing laws in Ireland (Tony Drummond); the Cork Traveller women's network (Louise Harrington & Michael Hayes); language, identity and interpretation (Ian Hancock; Michael Hayes; St. John Ó Donnabháin; David O'Donnell).

Multiculturalism is not new. What is new is the acknowledgement of diversity and multiculturalism within an emergent more cosmopolitan understanding and the necessity to create a dialogue between "mainstream" society, older minorities such as Irish Travellers and newer "immigrant" communities such as the Roma. A precondition for such cosmopolitan understanding to emerge is that the voices of Travellers and Roma are listened to and that their distinctive worldviews be provided with a platform for expression and that their input finds its way into policies that directly impact on their everyday lives. We hope that this volume makes some contribution towards the development of a more open and welcoming cosmopolitan European society. It is only through such a process that we may uncover a more critically productive discourse and understanding of the relationships that exist between Irish Travellers, Roma and the rest of Irish, British and European society.

Dr. Michael Hayes,
HEA Traveller and Roma Access Initiative, University of Limerick, Ireland
Dr. Thomas Acton,
Professor of Romani Studies, School of Humanities, University of Greenwich, London

CHAPTER ONE

HUMAN RIGHTS AS A PERSPECTIVE ON ENTITLEMENTS: THE DEBATE OVER 'GYPSY FAIRS' IN ENGLAND[1]

THOMAS ACTON*

Preface

This essay focuses on the annual Gypsy fair in Horsmonden, Kent. It charts the development of the fair and evaluates an attitudinal survey of village residents undertaken by the Gypsy Council, following moves by the local authorities to close the fair down. Unlike previous campaigns by Romani groups, which were cast in the discourse of ethnic exceptionalism, the campaign for Horsmonden represents a move towards the use of the human rights approach and the issue of non-discrimination by Romani activists. Instead of arguing for the continuation of a past privilege, the campaigners at Horsmonden defended the fair by claiming the right to freedom of assembly, based on the democratic support of the community where the fair was based. The use of an attitudinal survey to examine the opinions of non-Gypsies was novel; although sociological surveys have been used in Romani studies, in the past they generally entailed questionnaires aimed at Gypsies themselves, not at members of the community at large. The results of the survey showed that a majority of the villagers surveyed supported the continuation of the fair, in opposition to the local council decision to close the fair down. The general benefit and positive attitudes to the fair suggest that the refusal to allow permission for the fair grows out of racial prejudice and is not based on the general concerns expressed by the local community with regard to the fair.

---

[1] An earlier version of this paper first appeared in the Essex Human Rights Review 2004 Vol.1, No.1 pp 17-28 - http://projects.essex.ac.uk/ehrr/archive/pdf/46.pdf "Human Rights as a Perspective on Entitlements: The Debate Over 'Gypsy' Fairs in England" (Online: http://projects.essex.ac.uk/ehrr/)

Introduction

Within Great Britain the struggle to retain what are seen as 'Gypsy Fairs' is one of the earliest manifestations of collective political action by English Romani people, going back to the 1930s,[2] with battle being rejoined in the 1950s and 1960s.[3] Some of these gatherings were in fact dependent on large horse-racing gatherings, such as those at Epsom and Doncaster. Others are descended from medieval fairs and markets, which are no longer patronized by Gaje.[4] In the seventeenth and eighteenth centuries it was only possible for Gypsies to gather in large numbers without appearing threatening to the non-Gypsies at occasions when even larger numbers of non-Gypsies, strangers to each other, were present as a kind of cloak to the Gypsy gathering. Now, the Gypsy gatherings remain long after the non-Gypsy economy has moved on, and are defended as essential parts of Romani community life, for trade, culture and family life among those who are still nomadic and still seen as threatening when they gather together more than a few families.

Most of the earlier attempts by Romani groups to defend the continuation of these fairs were cast within a discourse of ethnic exceptionalism. They were defended as a part of tradition, as an exception to the normal rules of modern society, to be tolerated for the sake of an archaic community, rather than as the exercise of a normal human right to social and economic assembly. This paper will examine what may be the first political attempt to adopt a universalistic human rights approach to the defence of a fair, by the Gypsy Council at Horsmonden from 2001 onwards. The Gypsy Council, perhaps because the historical roots of this fair are believed to be only around a century old – it lacks any feudal documentation – sought to defend it by a direct appeal to the sympathies of the surrounding population, suggesting that it is a normal activity which brings, or can bring general benefits, and which no-one would think of opposing were it not for entrenched racial prejudice. This method – seeking to undermine the decision of political authority by appeal to democratic sentiments, as opposed to the supplication of authority to retain past privilege

---

[2] T. Acton, *Gypsy Politics and Social Change* (London: Routledge and Kegan Paul, 1974) 102.

[3] R.A.R. Wade, 'The Saving of Appleby Fair' (1966) XLV (1-2) *Journal of the Gypsy Lore Society* 29-39; R.A.R. Wade, 'A Travelling Traders' Guild' (1968) XLVII (1-2) *Journal of the Gypsy Lore Society* 29-31; and T. Acton, *Gypsy Politics and Social Change* (London: Routledge and Kegan Paul, 1974) 178.

[4] Gaje is the generalized plural Romani term for non-Gypsies. In the English Romani dialect it is pronounced 'Gaujos' or 'Gorjers'. The singular is 'Gajo'/'Gaujo'/'Gorjer'.

which has marked classic defences of fairs as by Gordon Boswell of Appleby[5] – has been linked to new intellectual methods of underwriting the political appeal – the adoption of contemporary social-scientific methodology in the form of a survey carried out by the Gypsy Council of local residents in a Kentish village.

This also marks out the human rights approach of the Gypsy Council as specifically anti-racist, where much traditional Gypsy politics remain enmeshed in special pleading. An example of the latter is the petition to the House of Commons from the Derbyshire Gypsy Liaison Group to write an ethnic definition of the term 'Gypsy' into the Housing Bill[6] to determine who can go on 'Gypsy Caravan Sites'.[7] This has been opposed by the Gypsy Council:[8]

The Gypsy Council believes that the right to reasonable choice of type of accommodation, and the right to stable and secure family residence within cultural tradition are human rights that all people, regardless of ethnicity, should enjoy. It believes, therefore, that well managed and designed caravan sites should in principle be allowed to be built on any land that is zoned for residential purposes. If, however, planning permission for caravan sites is to be restricted, priority should be given to those who travel as part of their occupation or economic, cultural or social way of life.[9]

---

[5] R.A.R. Wade, 'The Saving of Appleby Fair' (1966) XLV (1-2) *Journal of the Gypsy Lore Society* 29-39.

[6] 'The petition of the Derbyshire Gypsy Liaison Group and supporters declares that Gypsy people have for centuries been in the U.K. and that we are a distinct ethnic group sharing common ancestors, a distinct language, cultural beliefs and a common oral history. The Petitioners therefore request the House of Commons to introduce amendments to the 1/94 guidelines on planning and settlement applications to align them with the Mandla criteria of 1988 (*CRE v. Dutton*) in order to prevent racial discrimination against Romani and other ethnic Traveller peoples. The Irish Traveller community received ethnic status in 2000 (O'Leary).' The Derbyshire Gypsy Liaison Group, *Petition to Parliament* (2004).

[7] At present the definition of 'Gypsy' in planning legislation, following on from the 1968 Caravan Sites Act, despite its repeal, is 'a person of nomadic habit of life, regardless of ethnicity'.

[8] 'Asylum Seekers and EU expansion' Resolution Adopted at Gypsy Council AGM, Blackpool, 24 Apr. 2004 (Proposed: Thomas Acton, Seconded: George Wilson, all members present adopted the resolution); and 'Policy of the Gypsy Council on Site Planning Issues and Ethnicity' Resolution Adopted at Gypsy Council AGM, Blackpool, 24 Apr. 2004 (Proposed: Thomas Acton, Seconded: A. Bagehot, Andrew Ryder abstained but all other members present adopted the policy).

[9] 'Policy of the Gypsy Council on Site Planning Issues and Ethnicity' Resolution Adopted at Gypsy Council AGM, Blackpool, 24 Apr. 2004.

The Gypsy Council argues that the right to live in caravans must be a human right, not an ethnic privilege, and that the proper place to assert ethnic rights for Roma is in the Race Relations Act, or new anti-discrimination legislation, where everybody's ethnic rights are asserted as an element of their human rights, not as something peculiar to Gypsies:

The Gypsy Council calls on the Commission for Racial Equality and on the police to ensure that anti-discrimination laws are fully applied to end the present discrimination against Romani groups in access to residential and touring caravan sites, and in the operation of the planning process. It calls on the government fully to acknowledge the traditional ethnicity of Romani and Travelling groups within its policies for anti-racism, inclusion and diversity[10]

In this way, the debate between the particularistic Roma Rights approach, and the universalistic human rights approach finds a manifestation even in England.

Sociological Methodology and its Implications

It used to be part of the received wisdom that questionnaires would never work in research on Gypsies. Although the very first serious study of Gypsies in England[11] depended partly upon sending out questions to helpers, who visited Gypsy encampments in various parts of England to put those questions to the residents, this gave at best an outsider's view of their culture. Not until Goulet and Walshok put attitudinal questions to Spanish Gypsies in 1967-8 was modern survey methodology employed.[12] Even relatively recently, Okely, commenting on Mends'[13] use of a questionnaire in a study of Gypsy attitudes to Christianity in England, comments on its limitations:

There is little room for volunteered replies and comments. This is not to say that the questionnaire is by definition inappropriate, but whether used to interview minorities or majorities in the dominant society there are often severe limitations. It is best suited for large samples and simple questions where accuracy is more likely to be built in.[14]

---

[10] Ibid.

[11] J. Hoyland, *The Gypsies,* (York and London: W.M. Alexander, 1816).

[12] D. Goulet and M. Walshok, 'Values among underdeveloped marginals - the case of Spanish Gypsies' (1971) 13:4 *Comparative Studies in Society and History* 451-72.

[13] B. Mends, 'Researching the Religious Affiliations of Travellers and their Beliefs' in T. Acton and G. Mundy (eds.) *Romani Culture and Gypsy Identity,* (Hatfield: University of Hertfordshire Press, 1997) 158-63.

[14] J. Okely, 'Cultural ingenuity and travelling autonomy: not copying, just choosing' in T. Acton and G. Mundy (eds.) *Romani Culture and Gypsy Identity,* (Hatfield: University of Hertfordshire Press, 1997) 188-203 198.

In the same paper, however, Okely remarks how, during the Economic and Social Research Council Romani Studies Seminar at Greenwich University in 1993-4, Travellers who had read some of the gajé [sic] texts about their groups now, as self-ascribed members, were using outsiders' theories but trying them out in terms of their own identities and the wider political context within which Travellers have to survive.[15]

It might be objected that it is never clear where theories originate and whether they ever unambiguously belong to 'outsiders'; but, whatever their origins, Okely is right to suggest that scientific theory and methodology can never remain the exclusive property of one cultural group; they will be appropriated by whoever has a use for them. The present paper refers to what may be the first example, in Western Europe at least, of formal sociological research carried out by Gypsies on non-Gypsies, as opposed to the many examples the other way round.[16]

The initiative to do this arose out of the campaign by a loose coalition of Gypsy organizations led by the Gypsy Council, to keep Horsmonden Fair open in 2001. Although the present writer, a Gajo professional sociologist, was brought in at the stage when the first draft of the questionnaire was put before the Gypsy Council executive, and later helped with the analysis, the proposal and the distribution of the questionnaire were carried out by Gypsy members. Their objective was not in the first instance to put forward over-ambitious generalizations about Gajo-Gypsy relations in general, but the more modest one of trying to understand better the extent and nature of support for, and opposition to, the traditional fair in Horsmonden, and to use the facts they uncovered in negotiation with the local authorities. The research both uncovered a surprising groundswell of support for keeping the fair alive, and indicated various policies for eliminating sources of nuisance, such as bad parking, through a joint management committee, which were approved both by supporters of the fair and moderate opponents, and thus represented a way forward for compromise. It will be suggested that these have more general human implications for the relationship of social policy research to human rights action.

The questionnaire took the format of yes and no questions relating to the fair and further included a section regarding the demographic of respondents. The first section contained general questions regarding the respondents'

---

[15] Ibid.
[16] T. Acton, J. Lee, C. Smith and G. Wilson, *Studying the Gaujos: Using Social Science to Inform Romani Approaches to Local Communities* (unpublished report to the Gypsy Council, Aveley, Essex, 2003).

awareness of the closure of the fair, their attitude to its closure, and whether they felt consulted on the closure. There were further questions for those positive to the fair relating to potential improvement including: having fewer stalls on the green, having the horse parade through the village but keeping the main events in another place, and having a proper management group to run the fair. For respondents against the fair the questionnaire queried whether any other way of doing it would meet their needs, including reducing the size of the fair, holding all the horse events in another field, improving parking outside the village 'so that residents can live their own lives', and developing 'a more receptive management committee, which has Gypsy people, residents and police on it to make sure things are done better.' Finally, respondents were asked to give a number of details about themselves, including gender, age, ethnicity, occupation and home ownership.

Horsmonden Fair

The traditional fair at Horsmonden in Kent is not a 'charter fair', that is granted by an ancient royal charter, nor does it boast the antiquity of some other fairs. It is popularly believed to have grown out of a 19th century 'Hop-Pickers' Sunday', an event organized as recreation for casual agricultural labour, many of whom, of course, were Gypsies. When I first visited it in the 1960s it was small and had no 'amusements' such as roundabouts, but had a number of stalls selling china, shoes, curtains and cushion covers, and harness. It represented a serious shopping opportunity for many rural Travellers who fought shy of going to town centres. By late afternoon there would be a regular ebb tide of young mothers wheeling pushchairs laden with purchases back to their husbands, motors parked some way from the fair green at the outskirts of the village. The fair lasted only one day, so very few people except stallholders actually brought their trailers to stay overnight. There was also a fair amount of horse-trading. A small contingent of non-Gypsy evangelical Christians traditionally preached there in the days before the 'Light and Life' evangelical Romani movement spread to England. Over the years these were to be joined by stalls representing the Traveller Education Service (specialist teachers working with Roma/Gypsy/Traveller children) and even specialist Health Visitors (community nurses) working with Travellers.

As other fairs were closed down or threatened with closure, and as the English Gypsy community began to experience more prosperity after the 1968 Caravan Sites Act took the edge off earlier persecution, so Horsmonden fair grew during the 1970s to the point where there was justifiable concern about overcrowding of the small village green. At the beginning of the 1980s, the Romany Guild, another Gypsy organization, led by the late Tom Lee, negotiated with the local authority a shift of the fair to a large field rented from a farmer near Paddock Wood some miles away. At first this was a great success, with a considerable increase in the horse-trading and in the numbers of trailers staying overnight. Romanestan Publications even ran a bookstall there in 1983.[17] The Romany Guild, however, found it difficult to make a financial success of the fair, and ceded its administration to a smaller Kent-based organisation run by Tom Odley, an activist somewhat tainted by his association with the neo-fascist National Front.[18] Under Odley's direction the Paddock Wood fair shrank still further and was abandoned, leaving a few local Gypsies to gather back on the village green in Horsmonden. This much-reduced fair was quite successful, but its memory was marred by a fight which took place a fortnight after the fair in 1987 between some Gypsies and the one pub landlord who, in defiance of police advice, opened his pub. The incident is described vividly in a poem by Charles Smith.[19]

Although this incident was deplored by Gypsies and Gaje alike, it perhaps had the paradoxical effect of keeping some people away from the fair, and thereby keeping it smaller and more manageable. We can, in fact, see a kind of cyclical effect. When the fair is small, there is little trouble or nuisance, and the pleasant atmosphere causes the fair to grow. When it grows, there is more crowding and tension, which leads to trouble of some kind, and so the fair shrinks again. During the later 1990s it began to grow again, and opposition to it also grew.

The Biggest Stand-off with the Police since the 1960s

It is quite hard to ban an event that is not actually being organized by anyone, as was the case with Horsmonden Fair in the early 1990s. After the end of the Paddock Wood arrangement, Gypsies just turned up in hope with horses on the traditional day, and traders turned up in the hope of selling them – and the villagers – shoes, hot dogs and harness. The Parish Council could announce the fair was cancelled and place all the injunctions it liked, but unless someone were effectively to warn off the Travellers, they would still turn up, ignore notices, which often they could not read anyway, and at the end of the day the local authorities would still be organizing the clear-up. As they did so, Gypsy

[17] T. Acton and D. Kenrick (eds.), *Romani Rokkeripen Todivvus*, (London: Romanestan Publications, 1984) 6.

[18] Searchlight editorial, 'Racial Romany gets left-wing platform' *Searchlight,* 1989 March, 165:8.

[19] C. Smith, *The Spirit of the Flame* (Manchester: Manchester Traveller Education Service, 1990).

organizations, responding to complaints by Gypsies attending Horsmonden, started to campaign to keep it going.

In 2001, the local authorities made their most determined effort yet to stop the fair. Their strategy was to ask for an enormously-increased police presence, which was beyond the budget of the Kent Police Authority, while at the same time trying to legitimize their action by holding consultations with the Gypsy Council, who patiently undertook prolonged negotiations with the virulently opposed district and parish councils, and with the police, which failed to find a compromise. Finally the Home Secretary banned the fair by making the village an exclusion zone and authorized a huge police presence, in the end much greater and doubtless more expensive than the 'impossible' police presence that Kent County Council had refused to fund. Legal challenges to this failed, and one of the broadest coalitions of Gypsy organizations since the 1960s assembled to make a non-violent challenge to the exclusion zone on the day. Among prominent leaders were Charles Smith and Josie Lee, Chair and President of the Gypsy Council, and the late Eli Frankham, President of the National Romany Rights Association, while Grattan Puxon, the veteran former secretary of the International Romani Union, came out of retirement to co-ordinate publicity.

A massive number of police, estimated at between 600 and 700 officers, prevented perhaps half that number of Gypsies from entering the village. As a compromise the police agreed to allow 3 horses and wagons and a hundred marchers to go through the village, but at the point of entry they allowed only one horse and wagon, driven by Eli Frankham, and fewer than 50 marchers. Everyone else was left waiting impotently, horses literally champing at the bit, behind lines of police in helmets blocking off all access to the village.

Once through the police lines, however, the marchers did not encounter the hostility they had expected. Instead there were posters up in windows that said 'Save our Fair!'. As we progressed through the village people willingly took our leaflets and some asked if they could join us. Once a few did so, others joined them, some running into the houses and calling others. By the time we reached the end of our march the column of people was over 300 strong, with old age pensioners, mothers pushing toddlers in pushchairs, and young people walking and earnestly asking Gypsies present about Gypsy life. It was a beautiful day, and even the police relaxed as they realized that the villagers did not actually need protection, and there was no threat to public order, unless perhaps from villagers who resented the 'protection'. The overwhelming welcome of the villagers did more to take the sting out of the racism of the authorities than anyone could have thought possible. Only the other Gypsies, held back at police checkpoints with restive horses and small children sweltering in the hot sun, were still frustrated and unhappy, cut off from the little miracle of reconciliation happening inside the ring of steel.

It was this practical demonstration of support from the villagers that led the Gypsy Council committee[20] to decide to carry out a survey of residents as a way of helping them to communicate with the authorities, and of testing public opinion. A questionnaire was devised, then revised, and delivered with a stamped and addressed envelope for response to the 350 households living nearest to the village green which is the traditional site of the fair. There were 143 responses, a 41 per cent response rate, which is much higher than the normal response rate for a postal questionnaire, frequently as low as between 20 and 30 per cent.[21] Of these 143, eighty (56 per cent) took the trouble to write out their own additional comments, as well as responding to the close-ended questions. An absolute majority of seventy-nine (55 per cent) were against the closure of the fair, as opposed to forty-eight (34 per cent) who wanted the fair closed and sixteen (11 per cent) who could not make up their minds.

Who were these citizens of rural England who defied their parish council to welcome the Gypsies, and who were the ones who opposed the fair? Was it true, as many of those in favour of the fair wrote in their comments, that it was recent immigrants to the village, who were out of sympathy with old customs, who opposed the fair? And how strongly did people on both sides hold their views? An analysis was carried out using SPSS (Statistical Package for the Social Sciences) and using the Chi square test to measure the significance of association between variables.[22]

---

[20] The Gypsy Council includes both Gypsies and non-Gypsies in its subscription-based membership, and in its executive committee, although most of its office-holders, who initiated this research, are Gypsies.

[21] C.A. Moser and G. Kalton, *Survey Methods in Social Investigation*, (London: Heinemann, 2nd edn., 1971) Ch 11

[22] The 'statistical significance' of an association is the chance that it could have come about by chance if answers were given randomly. Where we say that an association is significant, we are using a sociological convention that there is less than one chance in twenty that we could have got the result in question by pure chance. Sometimes we give an actual 'significance value', a figure between 0 and 1. This is a precise statement of the chances that something could have come about by chance. For example the Chi square significance of the association between gender and broad occupational class categories was 0.010, which means that there are only ten chances in a thousand (or one in a hundred) that the differences in occupation found between men and women could have come about by chance.

The Respondents: The People of Horsmonden

The people who replied were probably not demographically unrepresentative, though a number of people, predominantly those against the fair, refused to give details of their age or gender, writing comments such as 'What difference does it make?'. Just under 20 per cent refused to state their sex, while just over 45 per cent were female and 35 per cent were male. So if it is true, as some methodologists suggest, that questionnaires given to households are filled in by the most powerful person in the household, then Horsmonden is not short of powerful women. There was, however, no significant difference between men and women in attitudes to the fair closure, or any other attitude questions, although it is interesting to note that the female respondents were significantly less likely to be higher professionals than men, and vastly more likely to be home-makers or housewives (no men reported themselves in this category). Fewer female respondents than male reported owning their home outright, but this difference was not statistically significant even at the 0.05 level. There is, however, a significant association between occupational class and home ownership. All the non-manual workers were home-owners, which was not true of any other occupational category.

Some 30 per cent of respondents reported owning their house outright, 25 per cent on a mortgage, 22 per cent were non-owners and 24 per cent failed to respond. That is, 71 per cent of those who answered this question were home-owners, not too dissimilar from national patterns. Those who did not own their own homes were significantly more likely to be over 68 or under 40 than any age group in between.

As a group, the respondents were older than the general population. Again, if that reflects on who in the house filled in the questionnaire, it shows that Horsmonden respects the wisdom of the aged as well as that of women. Setting aside the 23 per cent who felt their age was private, the remainder fell into four nearly equal age groups of 15-40 (twenty-eight), 41-52 (twenty-five), 56-67 (twenty-eight) and 68-88 (twenty-nine). Twenty-three per cent had lived in the village for less than 10 years, 22 per cent 11-20 years, 23 per cent 21-40 years, 17 per cent between 43 and 88 years, and 15 per cent refused to tell us how long they had been there. Those over 52 were significantly more likely to be manual workers than those in younger age groups.

The Gypsy Council had its own criticism of the simplified and rather racist ethnic labels used in the official British 2001 census, which did not encourage Romani people to state their ethnicity, and which included 'White' as an ethnicity. Rather than force such pre-defined racist ethnic labels onto respondents, as the census did, the Gypsy Council decided to ask respondents how they defined their own ethnicity. This, however, puzzled many of the respondents. Nearly half (46 per cent) left the question unanswered. Some (around 11 per cent) gave answers that might be described as ideological, describing themselves as 'anti-racist' or 'same as everyone else' or gave their religion. Some 13 per cent described themselves as British, 10 per cent as English and 13 per cent as White (14 per cent if we add the 2 who described themselves as Caucasian). Only eight people (5.6 per cent) gave any other ethnicity, including Irish, Celtic, South African, Iranian and two respondents who declared themselves 'Romany' (there are more Romani residents of Horsmonden, but they tend to live on the outskirts.) So those who would conventionally be defined as from an ethnic minority were very few. Nonetheless we shall see that how people defined themselves or did not define themselves in terms of ethnicity shows significant association with their attitudes. It also showed an association with their age. Younger people were significantly more likely to call themselves 'White'. Of those who described themselves as British only two were aged under 53, whereas half of all those who described themselves as White or Caucasian were in the youngest quartile, under 40. (Other ethnic categories were more evenly spread.) It is also interesting that no manual workers described themselves as 'White'. This generational shift in subjective ethnic identification had a knock-on effect on home ownership figures: The 'British' were four times more likely to own their homes outright than still be paying a mortgage, while 'White' home-owners were six and a half times more likely not to have paid off their mortgages yet. Nonetheless, as we shall see below, both categories are more likely than those who self-identify as 'English' to support the fair.

Attitudes: For or Against the Fair?

Simply counting up the numbers for or against the fair would produce a misleadingly polarized view of the village. There are only a small number of people on either side who hold their views so strongly that they are actually hostile to the other side. The overwhelming majority are prepared to compromise, and show this in their written comments. Those who are for the fair often want to see concessions made on parking, on limiting the size of the fair; those who are against the fair are mostly prepared to say that if these same concessions were really implemented then the situation would be much better. We can see the size of this moderate majority if we look at things that most people agree upon, whether they are pro or anti.

The most important of these is that if the fair is to continue, there needs to be a balanced management committee with representation by all interested parties, including the Gypsy Council. Of the 75 per cent who answered this question, those against the fair were 73 per cent in favour; those for the fair were 97 per cent in favour. Just five antis and two pros said no to this. Also, of the ninety-three who answered the question on parking, an overwhelming 88 per cent were in favour of better parking outside the village, with only two antis and nine pros dissenting.[23] These are the absolute diehards on both sides; those who thought that any acknowledgment of Gypsies was a step too far, or who thought the fair was too wonderful to need managing and any change would be unnecessary interference. They were not more than 10 per cent of the whole; the great majority wanted a harmonious solution, and believed that more could be done to achieve it. While it is true that those who agreed with the fair were significantly more likely to feel they had not been consulted about the fair, 43 per cent of those who wanted the fair closed also felt they had not been consulted. Some 75 per cent of the total answering this question felt they had not been consulted.

On other questions about what might improve the fair there was no general party line, and a much higher level of 'don't knows', between 30 and 50 per cent. Of those who did answer, 52 per cent were in favour of a smaller fair, and 55 per cent were in favour of having fewer stalls on the green. Forty-two per cent were in favour of having a horse parade in the village but putting other activities outside, while 46 per cent were in favour of putting horse events outside the village. Only on the last of these issues was there any significant association with overall attitudes to the fair's survival: only 12 per cent of those who were against putting the horse events in another field outside the village came from the anti-fair camp, but they were 36 per cent of those who did want to move horse events in this way. The Chi square significance of this association was 0.007 (only seven chances in a thousand it could have come about by chance), but still it must be noted there are dissenting minorities in both camps.

So the issues that seemed to command general consensus were the improvement of parking, and the setting up of a management committee. Another issue that might have brought a similar response was the need for more support for the clear-up after the fair; this was mentioned in many of the comments. As for other issues – well, that would be for a management committee to work out what would be for the best.

---

[23] Curiously there was a small but definitely significant association (Chi square significance 0.012) between the gender of respondents and support for parking outside the village: women were 96 per cent in favour, whereas men were a mere 79 per cent in favour.

Who was for and who was against the fair? We have already said there was no significant association with gender. Equally there was no significant association with home ownership status.

When it comes to age, the only significant association is that those who refused to tell us their age were far more like to be against the fair (by three to one). Almost half of those who refused to tell their age said they felt they had been consulted about the closure of the fair, significantly more than any declared age group. Amongst those who did tell us their age, the balance of antis and pros was almost the same in each age group, drifting slowly down from around a third of the youngest age group being against the fair to around a quarter of the oldest age group.

A similar picture can be seen when we ask how long people have lived in Horsmonden. Those who say they have lived in the village less than 20 years are around 61 per cent in favour of the fair; those who have lived in the village between 21 and 40 years are 80 per cent in favour, while among those who have lived in the village between 41 and 88 years, the majority in favour falls to 72 per cent; those who refuse to say how long they have lived in the village are 78 per cent against the fair. If we do some sums, and look at the differences according to the proportion of peoples' lives they have spent in the village, or cross-tabulate support of the fair with the number of years they have lived outside the village, then there is no significant association.

In other words, although a number of written comments by those for the fair suggest that those against it are mean-spirited recent arrivals, the evidence does not support this. It may be that there are one or two relative newcomers who are high- profile opponents of the fair, but other newcomers should not be judged by their example; equally there are one or two very longstanding residents who are against the fair.

When it comes to occupation, there are some weak but significant associations. The only group where there is a majority against the fair is again those who refused to state their occupation, but only about a fifth of manual workers and the retired are against the fair as opposed to around a third of non-manual workers and housewives.

The most interesting attitude differences are by respondents' self-ascribed ethnicity. As in all the demographic questions, the only majority against the fair (by thirty-one to twenty-seven) is among those who did not answer the question at all. But amongst the twenty-one people who put themselves in an ethnic minority or gave a response in terms of religion or being anti-racist, only two people opposed the fair. Among those who called themselves White or Caucasian, or British, 29 per cent and 27 per cent respectively were opposed;

but this rose to 43 per cent among those who called themselves English. The Chi square significance of this table was 0.003. There would appear to be quite complex links and associations between how people think about their own ethnic identity and their attitude to the Gypsy fair, which would warrant further research.

Conclusion

Although the attitudes of those who did not respond may differ from those who did, they are unlikely to hold stronger opinions than those who did respond, or to negate our strongest findings.

We can say that Horsmonden seems fairly representative of an English rural village a little over 50 miles from the centre of London. It is, on the whole, a hospitable, moderate-minded place. It is a desirable place to live and outsiders are moving in, including small numbers from ethnic minorities. The incomers tend to be younger and better-off than some of those who were born in the village or have been local for longer, but actually the attitudes of most of the incomers are not so different from long-term residents. It is a place where the old are respected and women are assertive, even though conventional differences in gender-roles remain.

By and large it is welcoming to the Gypsy Fair. A clear 55 per cent majority were in favour and a 73 per cent majority thought they had not been consulted over the decision to close the fair; these majorities are even higher if one eliminates the 'don't knows'.   But both among pros and antis an overwhelming majority wants to see a sensible solution. Very few respondents can be described as hardened opponents – usually individuals with some particular bad experience. Some still remember the fight which happened in 1987, or a meeting at which some parish council members felt Gypsy Council representatives had been rude. On both sides there was a majority belief that more could be done, especially on parking and on clearing up afterwards, through better management, with a management committee representing all interested parties.

Sensitive and dedicated local councillors can make a difference. For example, trouble over a much larger fair at Stow in Gloucestershire has been defused by the patient and untiring work of Cllr. Vera Norwood, who had been for many years a member of the Stow Parish Council (now Town Council), and was Mayor of Stow (and also a member of the Gypsy Council executive). Like all other Stow Councillors, Cllr. Norwood stood for the Council as an independent. She was for many years an active member of the Conservative Party. Disillusioned by the Conservative stance on Romani and some other issues, Cllr. Norwood (who anyway dislikes party politics taking too much prominence in local government) stood in 2001 for the District Council against the official candidate and won. Subsequently she resigned from the Conservative Party. This is possibly the first time that someone refused an official candidacy for being too pro-Gypsy has gone on to win in such circumstances. She also joined the Gypsy Council committee some years ago, where she sits alongside its chair, Charles Smith, who was a Labour Councillor and was elected Mayor of Castle Point in Essex. Sadly, both Norwood and Smith lost their seats in 2003 - not at the height of their human rights struggles, but after the campaigns had abated.

It can still therefore be argued that there is mileage yet in a more universal human rights approach, which seeks to use normal politics to confront prejudice head on, rather than seeking to sidestep it through exceptionalist politics which sees prejudice as inevitable. The public spirit evident in the care and thoughtfulness with which so many people responded by writing long additional comments showed that people, both English/British, Romani or from other ethnic minorities, were genuinely concerned to reach the compromises which could make a success of the fair. By using social survey methodology, the Gypsy Council was also reaching out to villagers, saying 'We are human beings like you', rather than warning 'We are irredeemably different to you – please don't make us obey normal rules!' This difference of approach will become crucial as the Romani, Gypsy and Traveller organizations move on to confront the debates over revision of the law on caravan sites, housing and other accommodation.

References

Acton T. (1974) *Gypsy Politics and Social Change;* London: Routledge and Kegan Paul

Acton, T. and Kenrick, D. eds. (1984) *Romani Rokkeripen Todivvus*; London: Romanestan Publications

Acton, T. Lee, J. Smith, C. and Wilson, C. eds. (2003) S*tudying the Gaujos: Using Social Science to Inform Romani Approaches to Local Communities;* (unpublished report to the Gypsy Council, Aveley, Essex, (2003).

Goulet, D. and Walshok, M. (1971) 'Values among underdeveloped marginals - the case of Spanish Gypsies' *Comparative Studies in Society and History* 13:4 451-72.

Hoyland, J. (1816) *The Gypsies*; York and London: W.M. Alexander

Mends, B. (1997) 'Researching the Religious Affiliations of Travellers and their Beliefs' in T. Acton and G. Mundy (eds.) *Romani Culture and Gypsy Identity;* Hatfield: University of Hertfordshire Press, 158-63.

Moser, C.A. and Kalton G. (1971 , 2nd ed.) *Survey Methods in Social Investigation*; London: Heinemann
O'Leary (2000) The Derbyshire Gypsy Liaison Group, *Petition to Parliament* (2004).
Wade, R.A.R. (1966) 'The Saving of Appleby Fair' in *Journal of the Gypsy Lore Society* XLV (1-2), 29-39.
—. (1968) 'A Travelling Traders' Guild' *Journal of the Gypsy Lore Society* XLVII (1-2), 29-31.
Okely J., 'Cultural ingenuity and travelling autonomy: not copying, just choosing' in T. Acton and G. Mundy (eds.) *Romani Culture and Gypsy Identity,* Hatfield: University of Hertfordshire Press (1997) 188-203.
Searchlight (editorial), 'Racial Romany gets left-wing platform' *Searchlight,* 1989 March, 165:8.
Smith, C. (1990) *The Spirit of the Flame*; Manchester: Manchester Traveller Education Service

CHAPTER TWO

GYPSIES AND TRAVELLERS ACCESSING THEIR OWN PAST: THE SURREY PROJECT AND ASPECTS OF MINORITY REPRESENTATION

JAKE BOWERS

I'd went to a funeral for my Uncle Jobie and it occurred to me that all the old folk were dying and taking a lot of their history and culture with them.
—Janet Keet-Black, Secretary of the Romany and Traveller Family History Society, UK

From Oxford's Gipsy Hill and Windsor's Tinkers Lane to Worthing's Romany Road, the historical contribution of Britain's 300,000 Gypsies and Travellers is hinted at in place names across the southeast of England. Yet despite being here for at least 500 years, the history and culture of Britain's travelling peoples has rarely been visible within public museums, libraries and archives in the region. This essay describes a new and innovative project as recently undertaken by Gypsies and Travellers in Surrey where an attempt was made to remedy this fact. The project entitled **Roads to Your Past** was based at the Surrey History Centre and involved the collaboration of Gypsies and Travellers from a wide range of counties in south-eastern England. Funded by the European Union and the South East Museum Library and Archive Council the Traveller Project was designed to encourage greater access to the region's museums, libraries and archives for the region's large Gypsy and Traveller population. The project is the British contribution to a 3- year pan-European effort to remove barriers in accessing cultural heritage. The project involved a indepth survey of Travellers and Gypsies and their attitudes to the manner in which they had been represented (if at all) as a community in places such as museums and libraries in the past and how they would like to see their identity and culture displayed in future initiatives involving museums, libraries, archives and other public institutions. A desire to explore the potential of museums, galleries, archives and libraries to meet the needs of Travellers and Gypsies and to encourage greater access to such public institutions on the part of these minorities was one of the principal raison d'etre's behind this project as was the incorporation of the principles of Action Research to a study which would have a strong collaborative ethos as developed between both the Traveller and Gypsy community and the non-Traveller community. The researchers on this project were conscious from the very beginning of how easy it could be to fall into the trap of speaking of an 'us' and a 'them' in the context of a project such as this, with 'us' being, in this case - the staff of cultural institutions - and the "them" being Travellers. An us/them approach to such a project would have been considered counter-productive for a number of reasons. It would have suggested antagonism and hostility between two communities whose cultures and histories, while including many similarities, are also very different in many ways. An element of divisiveness would immediately be apparent where there ought to be only mutual understanding and cultural acceptance or conversely. The second pitfall that had to be circumvented was the danger in going to the other extreme and over-compensating in terms of the homogeneity that exists in relation to the history and representation of both Travellers/Gypsies and non-Travellers. Gypsies, Travellers, museums, Showmen, archives and libraries are all institutions and groups which are complex and diverse. None of these institutions or groups are easy to categorise or "locate" definitively and all incorporate a dynamic which cuts across both ethnic and class barriers.

This research revealed that there is another 'us' (perhaps without a 'them') out there, an "us" which assigns significance to different aspects of contemporary culture but nevertheless is nevertheless concerned to preserve, understand, commemorate, record, account for and celebrate our human past. While being firmly rooted in the needs and concerns of Travellers, many of the themes and concerns identified by the Travellers and Gypsies who undertook this research echo concerns and issues that are current in many cultural institutions. These concerns are wide-ranging and include such issues as the ethical questions of ownership, the rights to interpret particular cultural phenomena and present aspects of them to the greater public and the practical questions of preservation methodologies, and classification terminology. One of the most important outcomes of this research was the usurpation of the "myth" that Gypsies and Travellers are communities which are "difficult to reach". The research demonstrated the opposite in fact. The overwhelmingly positive response to this research showed that there is both a phenomenal need and a desire within the community to share and preserve its history. Unfortunately, there is also a quite uniform experience of being ignored by museums, libraries and archives.

The settled population, who can make very little link between the romantic images of the past and the deprived and excluded images of the present, are also denied opportunities to learn about and interpret this recent history. While at times British Gypsy history may have been a painful and controversial story it is without question that it is still an important part of the national narrative.

Cognisant of the importance of collaboration between both the Traveller and Gypsy and the non-Traveller communities, it was noteworthy that a Romani journalist and writer Jake Bowers was employed as the project's researcher. His work began with identifying collections currently held within the region's museums, libraries and archives. He went on to consult members from all of the region's travelling communities: English Romanies, Romani refugees, Irish Travellers, New Travellers, Showmen and Circus People, about how best to preserve and celebrate the unique heritage of travelling people. It is hoped that his research, as outlined in this essay will act as a catalyst for the implementation of plans and guidelines as reagards the future work of museums, libraries and archives in the area. At a time when anti-Traveller hostility is on the rise, it is extremely important to recognise the long history of travelling people in the south-east of England. This project was not only designed to celebrate that history but to make it more accessible and visible in a way that was informed by the community itself. A central aim of the project was the hope that it would lead to the development of further and increasingly innovative pilot projects that would encourage more Gypsies and Travellers to explore their history, thereby creating an enhanced understanding in the wider community about all of Britain's nomadic cultures. The fact that there is strong evidence to suggest that Gypsies and Travellers represent the largest ethnic minority in counties such as Kent, Hampshire and Surrey and are also significant minorities in many other south-eastern counties made the objectives of this research even more crucial.

Research Methodology

The research consisted of two primary elements: research within the existing museums, libraries and archives community to identify current good practice, and action research within the community to identify ways of building upon this good practice. Existing good practice was documented where possible as tangible examples of how Gypsy and Traveller heritage is currently preserved, celebrated and represented. The current good practice served as a departure point from which to develop innovative ideas to further improve the representation of Gypsy and Traveller culture within the region's museums, libraries and archives. Research in conjunction with the Traveller and Gypsy community consisted of two aspects. An initial series of qualitative, in-depth interviews with leading Gypsy and Traveller activists, historians, family history researchers and craftsmen focused on common themes and ideas about how those already looking at heritage issues would like to see the Gypsy and Traveller heritage work develop. It is these insights that are the primary focus of this essay. This initial series of interviews was followed by a second series of quantitative interviews which, while less thematically-specific were more wide-ranging and consulted Gypsies and Travellers of all ethnic backgrounds and accommodation situations in all south-eastern counties about how the commu-nity would like to see its history and culture preserved and represented. The quantitative research also examined existing use of and attitudes towards museums, libraries and archives in order to provide a baseline with which to judge whether long term work has been successful. Half of these 100 interviews were done by the author, but the other 30% were done by the Traveller Education Service or other local authority staff in an attempt to increase the sample size, geographical coverage and statistical validity. A further 20% of results were gained through sending the questionnaire out to members of the Romany and Traveller Family History Society (RTFHS). The responses from all quantitative interviews were recorded anonymously. The ethnic background, sex, age and accommodation status were recorded however to ensure that the research was balanced and broadly representative.

Qualitative Stage

Before the beginning of this research personal experience suggested that while public museums, libraries and archives have already gone some way to engaging Gypsies and Travellers, the greatest work by far to preserve the community's heritage had been done by private individuals and institutions. The qualitative stage therefore focused on in-depth interviews with a number of known "practitioners" in the area of Traveller and Gypsy cultural heritage.

These were:

—Janet Keet-Black of the Romany and Traveller Family History Society.
—Gypsy activist and author Len Smith who designed the Romany Museum at Paulton's Park in Hampshire.
—Gary, Obie and Frank Brazil who have received heritage lottery funding for their private Romany museum in Marden, Kent.
—Henry and Paula Elliott who are establishing a Romani museum in Cranbrook, Kent.
—Gypsy historian Simon Evans in Kent

All of these individuals live in the south-east England area and all of them with the exception of Simon Evans - who has done a lot to improve the representation of Gypsies and Travellers in museums and libraries - are from the Traveller or Gypsy community. The insight of this group who have not only helped invent the wheel of preserving Gypsy and Traveller heritage, but set it in motion, were invaluable in setting the agenda in this research. All ethnic and occupational Traveller communities were included in this research project although Roma refugees from Eastern Europe were not included - as although, they form a part of the wider Gypsy and Traveller community in Britain - their experience of being excluded from mainstream services differs from indigenous Traveller and Gypsy communities as a consequence of differences in lifestyle and national origin. The communities were:

—English Romanies
—Irish Travellers
—New Travellers
—Showmen

Travellers in houses

The south-east is home to the second highest population of Gypsies and Travellers according to the Office of the Deputy Prime Ministers Bi-annual Caravan Count.[1] Despite being recognised as separate ethnic minorities under British race relations legislation (by a decision of the Court of Appeal: see Commission for Racial Equality v Dutton, Court of Appeal, 1988), English Gypsies and Irish Travellers are absent from the census and most forms of ethnic monitoring. An estimated 50% of all Travellers and Gypsies are now housed, either through choice, or often through a lack of accommodation. Statutory and voluntary services are primarily targeted towards Travellers living in caravans however irrespective of whether these Travellers are living on the roadside or on private or public sites. They are, after all, the most visible part of the Traveller population, but like the tip of an iceberg they do not represent what lies beneath the surface. In some respects this approach is understandable. Traveller Education Services, for example, specifically target Travellers living in caravans or on Gypsy sites and have difficulty identifying housed Travellers, frequently because they do not reveal their ethnic backgrounds to education authorities. In other cases, however, service providers are still very much using a gorgia (non-Gypsy) definition of what a Traveller is. That is, they are defined by their lifestyle (living in caravans) rather than by their ethnicity. But an English Romani or Irish Traveller does not lose their culture and heritage as soon as they move into housing. Research - (see Power, 2004 for example) - suggests that Travellers in housing are often more vulnerable to ill health[2], racist abuse, isolation and assimilation.

Travellers in housing also appear to be live at either end of the wealth spectrum. They are either in houses because they are wealthy enough to buy their own houses and have chosen to live that way, or they have been forced into social housing. Whether in housing through choice or compulsion, Travellers in housing are often in the most urgent need of service provision and arguably have the most to gain from accessing and celebrating their cultural heritage. They are isolated from their community, unable to live a traditional lifestyle, and sometimes, because of this, in conflict with those around them. For many in housing, the picture is bleak and their accommodation is perceived as a very real attempt to assimilate them into mainstream gorgia (non-Gypsy) society. It was a

---

[1] For more information on the Biannual Gypsy Caravan count see:
http://www.odpm.gov.uk/stellent/groups/odpm_housing/documents/page/odpm_house_0 27373.hcsp
[2] For more information on the ill-health experienced by Gypsies and Traveller in England please see the University of Sheffield report "The Health Status of Gypsy Travellers in England." Available at: www.shef.ac.uk/scharr

central remit of this research, therefore to consult with Gypsies and Travellers in housing as part of a conscious attempt to include the hidden majority within an invisible minority. 35% of the Travellers and Gypsies interviewed were men while 65% were women. 14% were under 16, 17% were aged between 17 and 30, 41% were between 31 and 45, 27% were between 46 and 65, and 1% were over 65. In order that the research could be made available on a collaborative basis with all Travellers and Gypsies within the survey whether the Travellers in question had a history of literacy or not it was decided to present the research in two forms: the written research, aspects of which are outlined in this essay and in audio form.

The use of audio for the presentation of the research was a new and relatively innovative approach with which to work with a minority where many among the older generation have limited literacy skills, but still need to be informed of the results. The audio report has given the community ownership of the research and allowed them the opportunity to press for the implementation of its recommendations. The written report, audio interviews and the photographs were taken have also being incorporated into a DVD used throughout Europe to train heritage professionals as part of ACCU: Access to Cultural Heritage, an EU wide project looking at removing barriers in accessing cultural heritage.

A travelling 'Egyptian' blacksmith being chased from a village.
Metal work remains an important trade for some Gypsies and Travellers.
Photo from 'Stopping Places: a Gypsy history of south London and Kent'
by Simon Evans.

Research Findings

This research has looked at two basic issues: the community's experience of how it has been served by museums, libraries and archives in the south-east in the past, and the way in which it would like to be represented in the future. However, none of this can be discussed in isolation from Gypsy history in England since it is this very history that has informed the experiences, views and attitudes recorded in this report.

A short Gypsy history

Ever since Gypsies arrived in Britain in the 16th century we have aroused fear, loathing and occasionally fascination. When Henry VIII sat on the throne, the penalty for simply being a Gypsy was execution. The 1554 "Egyptians Act" forbade Gypsies from entering England and imposed the death penalty on those of us who remained in the country for more than a month. The earliest British record relating to Gypsies that has as yet been found and relates to Surrey. It is dated the 1st of March 1569. A copy of a letter sent from the Privy Council to William More describes Queen Elizabeth's concern at disorders created by a "universal negligent and wilful permission of vagabonds and sundry beggars commonly called rogues and in some parts Egyptians [Gypsies]."[3] In October of the same year, a letter from the Privy Council to the High Sheriff and Justices of the Peace in Surrey, orders that "Egyptians" and other rogues be arrested and treated as vagabonds "whereby they may be driven by punishment to change that wicked and dangerous form of life."[4]

In more enlightened times, the death sentence was reduced to transportation. The 1597 Vagrancy Act made it possible for those that "will not be reformed of their roguish kind of life" to be conveyed to "parts beyond the seas". Nowadays, official policy towards Britain's travelling population recommends "toleration". The relationship between Britain and its Gypsy population has come a long way in five centuries, but it still has a long way to go. Many within the community feel its time our culture was not just tolerated, but celebrated. The twentieth century saw a rise in the conflict between Britain's nomadic and settled population that has still to be resolved. Despite the widespread and continuing closure of traditional stopping places, enough common land survived the centuries of enclosure to provide enough lawful

---

[3] Reference is located in the Loseley Manuscripts, Surrey History Centre, Woking. Reference: 6729/11/52 4 Surrey History Centre reference: LM/COR/3/561.
[4] Reference is located in the Loseley Manuscripts, Surrey History Centre, Woking. Reference: 6729/11/52 4 Surrey History Centre reference: LM/COR/3/562.

stopping places for people whose way of life was or had become nomadic. But in 1960, the Caravan Sites and Control of Development Act gave local authorities the power to close the commons to Travellers, which many proceeded to do with great energy. In the 1960s the pressure for the continual eviction of Gypsies with bulldozers and private security firms reached crisis point. In 1964 the leader of the Labour group on Birmingham Council called for "the extermination of the impossibles". After a wide-ranging campaign of resistance to evictions, a new Caravan Sites Act was passed in 1968, ordering local authorities to provide sites for all Gypsies residing in or resorting to their areas. For the first time in 500 years, the British state had recognised its responsibility to provide secure, legal stopping places for British Gypsies.

Few non-Gypsies have ever visited an official Gypsy site. Many epitomise the definition of a ghetto – a racially segregated and enclosed settlement. Many have been built near rubbish dumps, sewer works or noisy industrial facilities. In 1994, the situation for Gypsies and Travellers grew worsened considerably when the Criminal Justice and Public Order Act removed the legal obligation to provide even these sites. As a result, some local councils have privatised and closed many of the legal stopping places available to Britain's travelling population. Government policy currently recommends that travellers should house themselves. But Gypsy families that attempt to live on their own land are often denied planning permission. Over 80% of planning applications from settled people are granted consent, while more than 90% of applications from Gypsies are refused. The current conflict over "illegal" Travellers sites is in part caused by this history.[5]

Within the past fifty years the Gypsy and Traveller community has experienced dramatic and often traumatic change as economic change and draconian legislation have undermined its traditionally nomadic way of life. The community's role as agricultural labourers has declined due to mechanisation and the importation of cheaper eastern European and asylum seeker labour. Yet despite the huge upheavals, the community has done its best to preserve its own heritage with the resources it has had at its disposal. Whenever genuine requests to explore and represent that heritage have come from outside the community they have been enthusiastically responded to. Until now the various efforts to record have primarily. Space constraints necessitate that it would not be possible in this essay to to do justice to some of the best examples of that work which has been done to date to preserve and celebrate Gypsy and Traveller heritage in the South-East of England. It is a subject which I hope to devote a future essay to. It is only necessary here to outline a few of the motivations of the many Gypsy people who have already done trojan work to preserve the

---

[5] See Clark and Greenfield (2006) and Power (2004).

communal memory of their communities and the previous generations who went before them.

****

Janet Keet-Black

"We [the Romany Traveller and History Society] collect as much material as possible from the archives. But also from the community, simply because we feel it is important before it is all lost. There's an awareness amongst a lot of Gypsies and Travellers that they do want to know about their history and culture now."

Why have you done this?
"Because I'd went to a funeral for my Uncle Jobie and it occurred to me that all the old folk were dying and taking a lot of their history and culture with them. So I decided that I wanted to find out as much as I could before they all went."

What have you achieved so far?
"A lot. I think we've given a lot of Travellers the confidence to go in and do a bit of research themselves. And we've given the older Travellers an opportunity to get together and talk about the old times at our open days." [Janet Keet-Black, Romany and Traveller Family History Society]

Len Smith

Len Smith is an English Traveller, is originally from Yorkshire but has lived in the New Forest area for the nearly fifty years now. For most of his working life he has made his living as a carriage-builder. As part of that trade he also sometimes constructed Gypsy and Traveller and restored them. As he was interested in restoration work and had the necessary skills he got involved with Paulton's Park, a visitor attraction near Romsey, Hampshire where a big Romani exhibition has been established.

Why have you done this work – why has it been important to you?
" [This work] has been important to me because locally in the New Forest for instance Gypsies were accepted for hundreds of years and yet in more recent years had to endure a lot of discrimination. But more to the point, my grandparents were the ones who talked to me about Romani life and culture and trade practices and things like that."

What do you feel that you've achieved?
"Well although in one sense there's a disappointment in so far as this exhibit is all totally rooted in the past. But what it has achieved, is it teaches a lot of young traveller kids and the settled community about Gypsy and Traveller culture, what the way of life was like in the past, and with a history it helps reinforce your identity. Plus the huge numbers of people that go through this exhibit every year running into hundreds of thousands. Then if you only change the perceptions of even 1% of those people it makes a very big impact."

What more would you like to do?
"In general I'd like to see something much more rooted in the here and now, the problems that gypsies and travellers are facing as well as the enjoyment of Gypsy and Traveller culture – I think you need to reflect the whole bracket of Gypsy life as it is in the here and now because I think British society is inherently racist largely because of ignorance. If you can remove that ignorance by the same stroke you remove some of the racism."

Conclusion

Gypsies and Travellers are sometimes referred to as a "hard to reach group". Gypsies and Traveller society is also sometimes referred to as a closed or secretive society. This research demonstrated that by employing Gypsy and Traveller researchers and their advocates, the community is not difficult to reach at all, provided it is approached in the right way and with the right motivations. The overwhelmingly positive response to this research shows that there is both a phenomenal need and desire within the community to share and preserve its history. The fieldwork required for this project has demonstrated an urgent need to preserve the memories, photographs and artefacts of older community members. These people have experienced an extreme transition in their lives which mirrors the often traumatic changes in lifestyle that the community has experienced. Some born into bender tents or horse drawn wagons have witnessed the forced ending of a nomadic way of life that had survived with a language and traditions that can be traced back to India a millennium ago. Now living in private and social housing or static council or private sites, they are the only ones that can make sense of their history and help their descendants adapt to a more sedentary future. That history and transition is also not a uniquely Gypsy experience, the settled population who can make very little link between the romantic images of the past and the deprived and excluded images of the present also need an opportunity to learn about and interpret this recent history. Because Gypsy history is also an important part of British history. It is not just the Gypsy and Traveller role as eternal outsiders that needs representation. So too do those aspects of their culture and history which saw them as integrated citizens who have operated businesses, fought in wars and represented Britain in sports and the arts. At times, British Gypsy and Traveller history may have been a painful and controversial story, but it is still a part of the national narrative. It has been said that the way a society treats its minorities is a litmus test of its civilisation. Therefore a refusal to accept this history into the mainstream is also a reflection of how willing British society is to face up to the question of WHO we are and WHAT we have done. This research has also demonstrated that the community feels its place at the heart of British heritage work is missing, and there is a desire to plug a gap. That desire represents a challenge to those involved in the representation and interpretation of British history, but it is a challenge that the Gypsy and Traveller community is quite happy to help meet.

> Museums, libraries and archives could be powerful places for us if we can make them accessible. The way to make them accessible is do something good and it will draw people in and that spreads out in a pyramid.You bring two people in, and they tell four people and the four people tell another four people and it can start giving Gypsies and Travellers a bit more pride - we have a private pride in our culture - we need a public pride. We need a public face to our pride.
> —Len Smith, English Traveller

References

Acton T.   (1974) *Gypsy Politics and Social Change;* London: Routledge and Kegan Paul

Clark, C. and Greenfield, M. (2006) *Here to Stay: The Gypsies and Travellers of Britain*; Hatfield : University of Hertfordshire Press

Hancock, I. (1987). *The Pariah Syndrome : An Account of Gypsy Slavery and Persecution;* Michigan: Karoma Publishers

Hayes, M. (2006) *Irish Travellers: Representations and Realities*; Dublin: Liffey Press.

Kreps, C.F. (2003) *Liberating Culture: Cross-cultural Perspectives on museums, curation and heritage preservation*; London: Routledge

Mayall, D. (1987) *Gypsy-Travellers in Nineteenth-Century Society*; Cambridge: Cambridge University Press

—. (2004) *Gypsy Identities 1500-2000. From Egipcyans and Moon-men to the Ethnic Romany*; London: Routledge

Posey, D.A. and Dutfield, G. (1996) *Beyond Intellectual Property: Towards Traditional Resource Rights for Indigenous Peoples and Local Communities*; Ottawa:International Development Research Centre

Romany Family and Traveller History Society - Homepage:

http://www.rtfhs.org.uk/

Power, C. (2004) *Room to Roam: England's Irish Travellers – a Report of Research*; London: Community Fund

University of Sheffield Report "The Health Status of Gypsy Travellers in England." Available at: www.shef.ac.uk/scharr

CHAPTER THREE

US LITERATURE AND POPULAR CULTURE AND THE IRISH-AMERICAN TRAVELLER: A CALL FOR RESEARCH

MARY BURKE

In recent years, scholars of Irish literature have begun to make amends for the previous lack of attention given to both the construction of Travellers in canonical Irish literature and the hitherto fore often marginalized oral and textual literature generated by writers and performers originating from the community itself. I am currently revising a book manuscript of my doctoral thesis on the literary representation of the Irish "tinker" (as the minority was generally referred to in nineteenth- and early twentieth-century Irish and British literature, the period and canons I examine), and this work has brought me into contact with a new and young generation of scholars in Ireland, Britain, and particularly, North America who are consciously striving to engender awareness of the cultural legacy created by the negative and romanticized stereotypes of Travellers veined throughout generations of canonical Irish texts. Such stereotypes were, somehow, invisible to critics considering Irish literature and culture until surprisingly recently. Moreover, such representation is currently being considered alongside the critical reassessment of the creative writings and memoirs of Travellers who have "written back" to dominant culture in recent years. Traveller writers who have come to critical attention include memoirist and Traveller Rights activist Nan Joyce, novelist of Irish Traveller and British Romany descent Juanita Casey, and contemporary Traveller activist and dramatist Rosaleen McDonagh. Moreover, the fact that the considerable and centuries-old body of Irish balladry and folklore was often both generated and appropriated by Traveller performers and storytellers has also gained much more scholarly attention.

This is not to imply that enough work on the representation of Travellers in settled culture or sufficient appraisal of the texts and oral literature and balladry generated by members of the community has been done by literary and cultural critics. Indeed, it is beyond argument that such work is only just beginning. However, although research concerning literature about and by the Traveller is still in its infancy, it is already leading to a greater awareness amongst Irish Studies scholars of the variegated nature of Irishness and the neglect of minority identities in considerations of the construction of "Irishnesses" in the literary text. Furthermore, the attention given by historians, folklorists, linguists, and literary scholars in recent years to the history, culture, language, and literary output of the Irish Jewish community and the Ulster-Scots tradition within the island of Ireland can only draw further attention to the shameful lacuna that has existed in scholarship concerning Ireland when it comes to considering what has been argued to be country's only indigenous ethnic minority. Such continuing calls for a broader, more nuanced, and more inclusive definition of Irishness can only assist in making instructors in Irish literature aware that diversity in the Irish canon is more than a simple matter of listing settled Irish authors writing in English alongside settled Irish-language writers on Irish literature reading lists! To give a sense of the recent groundswell of awareness in varieties of Irishness long neglected by mainstream linguistic and literary scholarship and the entwined nature of such interests, I can state with much satisfaction that on a recent (June 2006) two-week trip to Ireland during which I attended NUIG's First Galway Conference of Irish Studies: Orality and Modern Irish Culture, I heard a conference paper that considered "instances of Irish in Traveller Cant and Ulster-Scots" and spoke only a day later with a free-lance radio producer striving to have both Juanita Casey and a dramatist of the Ulster Literary Theatre (a kind of self-conscious Ulster response to the Abbey Theatre) included in a series on neglected but critically important Irish writers currently being pitched to RTE radio. Moreover, I can state with some pleasure that since I started attending and delivering papers at Irish, British, and North American Irish Studies conferences in 2001, the number of papers by scholars of literature and folklore considering both the representation of Travellers in canonical Irish literature and the literature of Travellers themselves has markedly increased. Most encouragingly, two conferences were organized on the island of Ireland since 2000 (one at Queen's University Belfast, the other at the University of Limerick) around the theme of Irish minority and/or Traveller culture, language and history, at which a wide variety of papers on the subject were presented by both Traveller and non-Traveller scholars, community leaders and commentators.

As an Irish researcher of wholly settled descent currently examining the issue of the construct of the Traveller in the Irish and British text and slowly nudging toward a basic understanding of the place of the literature created by the community within a broader Irish literary canon, my hope is that in the not-too-distant future, scholars of Irish Traveller descent within academia will themselves tackle these issues and the fundamental question as to whether published and/or literate Traveller writers should (as settled critics currently assume in their deliberations) be considered spokespeople for a culture that was, throughout most of its history, primarily oral and non-literate. (Although I am only gradually and patchily becoming aware of the history of African-American Studies since I have settled in the US and entered the American academy, I think it is safe to state that African-American culture and literature were not particularly visible to the mainstream American academy until professors from that culture or sensitive to that tradition started to make their voices heard and to challenge the dominant model of what constituted "good" writing.)

All this leads me to new questions I have been forced to confront since moving to the US in 2003. Although I have continued to engage with Irish culture and literature and with my specialized field of the literary construct of Travellers on a research and teaching level since arriving in North America, I have, of course, been immersed in much popular American culture in my everyday life and leisure time. I had little sense of the representation of the Irish-American Traveller in North American literature and popular culture (or indeed, that Travellers *were* represented in the culture) before moving to the US. Having lived in New England for a few years by now, I have become aware that despite the fact that Irish-American Travelers or Travellers (both spellings are used by members of the community itself) are a tiny and generally unknown minority, they are represented in US popular culture and fiction to a disproportionate degree. Six popular novels centred on the topic have come to my attention, as well as one relatively successful independent film, an episode of a popular detective television series, and a *whole* television series currently in production, the pilot episode of which is scheduled to be broadcast in the US in the autumn of 2006. Granted this is not an enormous volume of material, but it is a disproportionately large amount of material given that the minority has been numbered at 30,000 people.[1] Few minorities of comparable size can claim as much (possibly dubious) attention in American popular culture. Such wholly unexpected representation of what constitutes a tiny Irish-American minority population led me to a series of questions that I am not yet able to answer, but which will, I hope, be the kind of questions that will soon begin to be posed by a new generation of scholars interested in querying the established certainties of Irish-American history, culture, identity, and assimilation. (Of course, potential

---

[1] Ian Hancock, personal correspondence to Michael McDonagh and Robbie McVeigh, quoted in *Minceir Neeja in the Thome Munkra: Irish Travellers in the USA*, (Belfast: Belfast Travellers' Education and Development Group, 1996) 23.

researchers of settled descent hoping to engage with Travel(l)ers themselves must first confront and negotiate the reticence of members of the community in the face of scholarly interest with sensitivity and resourcefulness: requests for information about the community posted online in recent years have generally received little response. Given that a number of websites run by Irish-American Travel(l)ers about their culture exist and that the community is generally more literate and "wired" than the related Irish population group, this lack of response is not necessarily due to the fact that the postings by researchers requesting co-operation have gone unread by the target population.)

Before listing what I think are the questions that need to be addressed in order to begin to understand how the Irish-American Travel(l)er might be situated within broader research concerning Irish-America and Irish-American identity, I will first give a necessarily short sketch of the history of Travel(l)ers in the US as it is currently understood by anthropologists, contemporary folklorists and American educators who have had contact with members of the community. Given the dearth of research available on this subject, this pen picture, which synopsises the tiny available body of scholarship on the subject is, doubtlessly, extremely imprecise.[2]

Irish Travel(l)ers, descendants of the historically nomadic Irish Traveller community, with whom they share many cultural traits, constitute a small population of scattered groups that has resided predominantly in the southern states of America since emigrating from Ireland. Oral accounts suggest that eight Travel(l)er families, led by a pioneer named Tom Carroll (1830-1910), who is buried in Westview Cemetery, Atlanta, emigrated from either Ireland or England sometime between 1850 and 1865, and initially spread throughout the urban Northeast, where they practiced their ancestral occupations. Prior to the Civil War, Travel(l)ers had begun to winter in the southern states, where they very successfully traded mules and horses. When the demand for these animals decreased in the late 1800s, Travel(l)ers took up permanent bases in the South, and Travel(l)er males subsequently concentrated on providing linoleum peddling, spray-painting, tarmacadaming, and related services to farming

---

[2] My synopsis of the current research available on the Irish-American Travel(l)er minority is a paraphrase of the Irish Travel(l)er entry I have written for the forthcoming *Encyclopedia of Irish-American Relations*. Eds. Jason King, Philip Coleman, and Jim Byrne. California: ABC-CLIO, forthcoming. I would like to thank the editors for the permission I received to partially reproduce the entry. The following list of texts on which the synopsis is based is drawn from William G. Lockwood and Sheila Salo's *Gypsies and Travelers in North America: An Annotated Bibliography* (Cheverly, MD: Gypsy Lore Society, 1994).

communities, occupations that continue to this day. Since the 1960s, Travel(l)ers have abandoned the tents and trucks of previous generations for villages of luxury mobile homes and, increasingly, houses. Despite these adaptations to sedentary norms, business transactions continue to be cash-based, and trading and bartering are still used in dealings. Moreover, contemporary Travel(l)ers appear to have remained more seasonally nomadic than their Irish counterparts. Overall, Travel(l)er culture remains independent, self-reliant, and enclosed. American anthropologists generally describe Travel(l)ers in the United States as an ethnic minority, although this has yet to be acknowledged in US law. Like their Irish counterparts (with whom a certain degree of contact has recently emerged[3] despite the fact that no Irish-American Travel(l)er-specific organizations have been founded), Travel(l)ers in the United States share common descent, and have discrete cultural practices: boundary rules against most outsiders, a tradition of self-employment and involvement in trades or services not generally pursued by members of the settled community, a unique material culture, rigid and traditional gender roles, adherence to Catholicism involving public displays of religiosity, early marriage and substantial dowry payments when the families are sufficiently affluent, an aspiration to be mobile, customs surrounding cleansing, and a cryptolect traditionally used instead of or alongside English in certain situations. Moreover, the extended family was and remains the key unit of social and cultural reproduction. Travel(l)ers are generally markedly wealthier and better-educated than their Irish counterparts, making them less visible and liable to public scrutiny. The minority remained largely undocumented by serious commentators in the US until the 1970s. Academic studies of the community remain scant, due in part to Travel(l)er itinerancy and the aforementioned suspicion regarding researchers from majority culture. For these reasons, and also because the U.S. Census does not recognize Travel(l)ers as a unique ethnic group, population figures are unavailable. Ian Hancock, an expert in Romany culture based at the University of Texas at Austin, has made the estimate (quoted above) that there are upwards of 30,000 Irish Travel(l)ers in the US. Their existence is generally unknown or of little interest to the settled Irish.[4]

---

[3] In 1994, Irish Traveller activist Michael McDonagh accompanied the Belfast anthropologist Robbie McVeigh to Murphy Village, a Travel(l)er settlement of about 2000 people established in the 1960s near Augusta, South Carolina. See the resulting publication, *Minceir Neeja in the Thome Munkra: Irish Travellers in the USA*.
[4] For instance, the very first official report on the minority was only produced by the Irish Government in 1963, and although it claimed to be a comprehensive investigation of Traveller culture and lifestyle, no mention was made of the related community in the United States. My suspicion is that the relatively wealthy, educated and cohesive

When what little is known of Irish-American Travel(l)ers is finally fully considered alongside fictional, televisual and cinematic depictions of the community, it appears to me that the following questions will have to be addressed by researchers before the Irish-American Travel(l)er construct might begin to be uncovered and understood:

> Why is such a tiny minority subject to such a disproportionately large degree of attention from North American popular authors and scriptwriters?

> What are the common stereotypes invoked in such representation, and what kind of fantasy is generally projected onto a minority that remains essentially unknown to the average American?

> How do such depictions compare and contrast with the construct of Irish Travellers in Irish culture?

> Do Irish-American Travel(l)ers generate their own oral and written literature? If so, what is its relationship to the output of the related Irish community?

> Did the Travel(l)er initially come to attention in America as a variety of Irish immigrant or as a variety of "dark-skinned" Gypsy?

>> If the latter, where are contemporary Travel(l)ers placed within the racial binary of "black" and "white" that might be said to divide America?

>> Where do Irish Travel(l)ers fit within the generally homogenous identity of contemporary Irish-American, which appears to define itself as exclusively settled, Catholic, and urban?

>> Were and are Travel(l)er musicians a visible and discrete presence in the American folk-music scene?

In short, such fundamental and exploratory questions suggest that, much like the very new light being thrown onto established notions of Irish history and Irish identity now that "lesser" varieties of Irishness are finally being considered by scholars of Irish history and culture, the examination of Irish-American history, culture, identity, and assimilation requires a broadening of emphasis to include

---

American Travel(l)er community challenges comfortable stereotypes of the fecklessness, indigence and fractured nature of the related Irish population group.

other varieties of Irish-Americanness not currently examined. Incredibly, no volume of the many works on Irish-America and its history that I consulted in researching this necessarily short article listed even one entry on Travel(l)ers in the index.

References

Andereck, Mary E. *Ethnic Awareness and the School: An Ethnographic Study.* Sage Series on Race and Ethnic Relations, vol. 5. Newbury Park, CA: Sage, 1992.

Bond, Pat. "The Irish Travellers in the United States." *Sinsear: The Folklore Journal* 5 (1988): 45-58.

McDonagh, Michael and Robbie McVeigh. *Minceir Neeja in the Thome Munkra: Irish Travellers in the USA.* Belfast: Belfast Travellers' Education and Development Group, 1996.

Gmelch, Sharon. *Tinkers and Travellers.* Dublin: O'Brien, 1975.

Kent, Linda L. "Fieldwork That Failed." *The Naked Anthropologist.* Ed. Philip R. DeVita. Belmont, CA: Wadsworth, 1992, 17-25.

Kinch, Rita. Entry on Irish-American Travel(l)ers. *Encyclopedia of Irish America.* Ed. Michael Glazier. University of Notre Dame Press, 1999.

Harper, Jared Vincent. "'Gypsy' Research in the South." *The Not So Solid South: Anthropological Studies in a Regional Subculture.* Ed. J. Kenneth Morland. Athens, GA: Southern Anthropological Society, 1971, 16-24.

—. "Irish Traveller Cant." *Journal of English Linguistics* 15 (1971): 78-86.

Harper, Jared Vincent and Charles Hudson. "Irish Traveller Cant in its Social Setting." *Southern Folklore Quarterly* 37.2 (1973): 101-114.

Radharc: Stories from Irish America. "Travellers of Murphy Village." Transmitted on RTE (Ireland), April 23, 1995.

CHAPTER FOUR

KEEP ON MOVING, DON'T STOP NOW: ANTI-TRESPASS LAWS ON THE ISLAND OF IRELAND

TONY DRUMMOND

This research note is an updated version of a paper originally presented at the 14th World Congress of Criminology at the University of Pennsylvania Philadelphia in 2005. The findings here stem from my PhD studies at the University of Ulster concerning Irish Travellers' perceptions of and experiences with criminal justice across the island of Ireland.

Within this article, the consequences of the Housing (Miscellaneous Provisions) Act 2002 (HMPA, 2002) for illegally encamped Irish Travellers in the Republic of Ireland are discussed. Likewise, the implications of the Unauthorised Encampments (Northern Ireland) Order 2005 (UENIO, 2005) for illegally encamped Irish Travellers in Northern Ireland are presented.[1] In essence, whilst embodying the frustrations of the two state parties regarding control of illegal encampments on the island, the two pieces of legislation outlined above and discussed in detail below, encourage a critique of the failures of the two governments[2] with regards to these issues.

As will be demonstrated in due course, one of the crucial failures of state parties within both jurisdictions related to illegal encampments has been to

---

[1] The Housing (Miscellaneous Provisions) Act 2002 is commonly referred to by Travellers as the anti-trespass law. Soon no doubt, the same will apply to the Unauthorised Encampments (Northern Ireland) Order 2005. Neither the 2002 Act nor the 2005 Order name Travellers, yet in interviews the perceptions of Travellers and associated respondents were that these two pieces of legislation were deliberately targeted at the Traveller Community. Both pieces of legislation are also referred to throughout this article as the anti-trespass laws.

[2] At time of writing Northern Ireland is governed under the principle of direct rule and Orders are passed via Parliament in London. Devolved government of Northern Ireland is currently suspended.

record an accurate count of the Traveller population. Another failure posited here is that despite existing legislation in the Republic of Ireland and an official document in Northern Ireland indicating support for nomadism, adequate transient site provision has not been made for Travellers. The concern is then raised here that via evictions, state parties have reneged on their opinions regarding acceptance of and provisions for nomadism. The failure of the Republic of Ireland's government to concur with Northern Ireland's state policies regarding Travellers as a distinct ethnic minority and of the Garda Síochána[3] to follow the example set by the reticence of the Police Service of Northern Ireland (PSNI) in Northern Ireland (at least until 19/07/06) to become involved in enforcing anti-trespass legislation, is also presented and analysed. What is more, the implications for Irish Travellers on the island of Ireland of two recent key case human rights decisions concerning Gypsies and Travellers in England, are considered.

The Anti-Trespass laws

Despite protestations by Joyce (2003) and the Irish Traveller Movement that pre-existing legislation[4] was adequate enough to control illegal encampments, in the Republic of Ireland, Section 24 of the HMPA 2002 amended the Criminal Justice (Public Order) Act 1994, to provide for the offence of criminal trespass on public or private land (NTACC, 2004: 67). Concerns were also aired in the Republic of Ireland that the HMPA 2002 would be in opposition to equality legislation such as the Equal Status Act 2000.[5] The unprecedented effect of the HMPA 2002 is that Travellers can be moved on by Gardai with less than 24

---

[3] Irish police.

[4] In the Republic of Ireland, pre-existing legislation is as follows: Section 31 of the 1948 Local Government (Sanitary Service) Act provides for the prohibition and exclusion of Temporary Dwellings from Local Authority areas; Section 27 of the Planning Act 1976 is frequently used to seek injunctions preventing Travellers occupying caravans in many areas; Section 69 of the Road Act 1992 deals with the erection and maintenance of Temporary dwellings and gives the power of seizure to Garda and authorised persons to remove Caravans from certain types of roads and Section 24 of the Housing Act 2003 gives power of arrest and seizure to Garda where a Caravan is parked on public or private property without consent. In effect, all areas not covered by the Roads Act 1992.

[5] Under the Equal Status Act 2000 Travellers are defined as the Traveller community meaning the community of people who are commonly called Travellers and who are identified (both by themselves and others) as people with a shared history, culture and traditions including, historically, a nomadic way of life on the island of Ireland. The Act offers protection to members of the Irish Traveller Community as well as other named groups on grounds of access to services and goods in the Republic of Ireland. See: The Irish Statute Book.

hours notice. If Travellers refuse to move on, despite lack of alternative provision by the state, they may be arrested without the need for a warrant. Failure to comply with a Garda's request to leave an illegal encampment can result in Travellers receiving fines up to € 3000 or, being imprisoned for a month or both (TVG, 2003).[6] Moreover, caravans and vehicles may be impounded and charges are levied for each day that a vehicle or caravan is kept in storage.

The courts are rarely involved within the framework of the HMPA 2002 legislation as the Garda have extensive powers to decide when an offence has been committed. Moreover, the ITM (2003) revealed that the use of the HMPA 2002 is undocumented by the legislator, the courts and the executive. Between July 2002 (when the HMPA 2002 was implemented) and October 2003, over 150 evictions were recorded by the Irish Traveller Movement (Pavee Point, 2005; ITM, 2003).[7] The monitoring undertaken by the ITM suggested disruption to the educational, welfare and health provision of Travellers whilst severely impairing or destroying their chances of social integration.

In Northern Ireland, the UENIO 2005 had been suspended for almost a year due to concerns expressed by critics (ECNI, 2004) such as the Equality Commission for Northern Ireland regarding the original Draft Unauthorised Encampments (Northern Ireland) Order 2004 (DUENIO, 2004). The Equality Commission drew attention to the likely increase in the social exclusion of the Traveller Community that would be incurred by provisions within the DUENIO, 2004; the possible contravention of various international instruments,[8] and the fact that such legislation was likely to be both directly and indirectly discriminatory under current race equality legislation[9] and in opposition to

---

[6] On 18/1103, Judge Con O' Leary sentenced a Traveller and his wife to one month each in prison (suspended for two years). Along with their son, the three Travellers were also fined €1000 between them. The elderly man and his wife were the first two Travellers to receive suspended prison sentences for illegal encampment in the Republic of Ireland.

[7] In contrast, the NTACC (2004: 69) revealed that in answer to a Parliamentary Question in October 2003, the Minister for Justice, Equality and Law Reform indicated that up until that point the Act had been used on 88 occasions to evict Travellers. The ministers' reply is at odds with the ITM's calculations and also, the belief that evictions are *not* officially monitored.

[8] For example: Article 13 of the EU Race Directive 2000.

[9] For example: Section 75 of the NI Act 1998 came into force on 1st January 2000. It requires public authorities to have due regard to the need to promote equality of opportunity between persons of different religious belief, political opinion, racial group, age, marital status, or sexual orientation; between men and women generally; between persons with a disability and persons without; and between persons with dependants and persons without. Public authorities are also required to have regard to the desirability of promoting good relations between people of different religious belief, political opinion or

human rights (PSNI, 2003; PSNI, 2004 NIHRC, 2004; NICVA, 2004; ECNI, 2004). As in the case of concerns raised by the ITM (2003) related to the HMPA 2002 in the Republic of Ireland, the Equality Commission accentuated the range of civil law currently used to successfully remove unauthorised encampments[10] in Northern Ireland and strongly recommended that the Department of Social Development abandon the proposal for the DUENIO, 2004.

Regardless of the above concerns, on 09/6/06 the Social Development Minister for the Northern Ireland Office David Hanson, announced that the UENIO 2005 would be sanctioned on 19/07/06. Akin to the effects of the HMPA 2002, under the UENIO 2005, police will be given the unprecedented power to seize the vehicles of those (Travellers presumably, who else is nomadic?) who camp illegally if they refuse to comply with an order to leave the land. Under the conditions of the UENIO 2005 Travellers could also face jail and a fine of up to £2500 for refusing to leave an illegal camp. Basically, the UENIO 2005 mirrors the provisions contained within the HMPA 2005 in the Republic of Ireland. Minister Hanson stressed however, that Travellers would be protected by a requirement that in the first instance, police must make enquiries as to whether or not the Housing Executive for Northern Ireland could provide alternative sites for Travellers to turn to[11] (UTV, 2006). In a follow up to these developments, on the 15th July, Minister David Hanson revealed that police will be able to move Travellers on to a registered site, which will be open and operational by the end of July (BBC News, 2006). However, in answer to this prophecy, Derek Hanway, managing director of Belfast Traveller support group An Munia Tober[12] stated:

> We are not sure where that site is, and it is not acceptable that the minister, at 4 o'clock on a Friday, shoots off a press release to say that this legislation is coming in on 19 July and that's it (BBC News, 2006).

As indicated so far, despite sanctioning the HMPA 2002 and the UENIO 2005 the fact remains that there is a grave lack of accommodation provision for

---

racial group. The definition of Irish Traveller is based upon terms in the Race Relations (Northern Ireland) Order 1997 explicitly referring to Irish Travellers as: the community of people commonly so called who are identified (both by themselves and by others) as people with a shared history, culture and traditions including, historically, a nomadic way of life on the island of Ireland.

[10] In Northern Ireland, pre-existing legislation is as follows: the Public Health (Ireland) Act 1878, the Housing Act 1963, the Pollution Control and Local Government (Northern Ireland) Order 1978 and the Roads (Northern Ireland) Order 1980.

[11] As of June 2006, there are **no** transient sites in Northern Ireland.

[12] Meaning: the good road in the Traveller language/dialect of Cant.

Travellers (including transient sites) across the island (ITM, 2003; ECNI, 2004). As detailed below, a lack of accommodation has been exacerbated by lack of precise figures concerning the population count of Travellers.

A Contested Population

At the close of 2004, the Department of the Environment, Heritage and Local Government (DEHLG) *estimated* that there were 6,991 Irish Traveller *families* recorded as residing in the Republic of Ireland.[13]   Although it is unhelpful that families, as opposed to individuals were counted, the guesstimate of the DEHLG implies that the population count of Travellers in the Republic of Ireland (families multiplied four times) would be approximately 28,000.   Yet, David Joyce of the Irish Traveller Movement disputed the figures provided by the DEHLG believing it more likely that there were at least 40,000 Travellers residing in the Republic of Ireland.[14]   Recently, a report by Unison (2006) confirmed that the population count of Travellers remains ambiguous revealing that: '[t]he first true indication of the number of Travellers in [the Republic of] Ireland could become clear after this weekend's [2006] census' (Unison, 2006: 1).   The disputed Traveller population count indicates that even if the state of the Republic of Ireland were to provide more transient site accommodation, provision would not necessarily equate to need.

The fact that as with the case in the Republic of Ireland, there remains a serious shortfall in all types of Traveller accommodation provision in Northern Ireland was recently affirmed when the Chief Executive of the Northern Ireland Housing Executive (NIHE) Paddy McIntyre, admitted in a statement that:

> There is still a long way to go in respect of meeting the accommodation needs of Travellers but I remain confident that through partnership working the various statutory organisations will continue to tackle social disadvantage within the Traveller Community (NIHE, 2005 b: 1).

In answer to my question regarding the population count of Travellers in Northern Ireland, Aidan Brannigan of the Traveller Project Team, NIHE revealed that their population can only be estimated at around 1200-1500. Also he stated that: 'Due to their nomadic lifestyle it is difficult to put an exact figure

---

[13] According to figures collected within the Annual Count, 'Traveller Families in Local Authority Assisted Accommodation and on Unauthorised sites' which took place on the 26/11/04.   Written reply received from Danny Mc Elhinney, Traveller Accommodation Unit, the Department of the Environment, Heritage and Local Government, 04/05/05.

[14] Email communication estimating population count based on large Traveller family size eg. 6-8 persons per family, received from David Joyce of the Irish Traveller Movement, Dublin, 02/06/05.

on the number of Travellers resident in Northern Ireland at any given time'.[15] Thus, it appears that as is the case in the Republic of Ireland, a lack of accurate statistics can only impede development of accommodation (including transient site) provision.

Despite the contested population count of Travellers, the fact that the HMPA 2002 was passed in the Republic of Ireland and the UENIO 2005 has been given a green light in Northern Ireland is of interest in consideration of pre-existing official support for provision of transient sites across the island.

Official Support for Nomadism

Prior to sanctioning of the HMPA 2002 in the Republic of Ireland, both the Housing (Traveller Accommodation) Act 1988 (HTAA 1988) and the Housing Act 1998 (HA 1998) provided that the housing authority must, in the first instance: 'make further provision for transient and temporary sites...' and in the latter case "have regard to' the need for transient halting sites.....'[16] Despite the recommendation contained within the HTAA 1988 and awareness of the need for transient site provision in the HA 1998, as of June 2006 only two official transient sites existed in the Republic of Ireland.[17]

In contrast, in Northern Ireland in 1996, the Department of the Environment for Northern Ireland had established a working party to consider the accommodation needs of Travellers up until 2006. In the final report of this venture under the title: 'Accommodating Nomadism' it was revealed that: '[T]he Race Relations (NI) Order 1997 not only defines Travellers as a specific 'racial group' but identifies nomadism as a key aspect of their cultural identity.' Moreover, it was recommended that:

> Not only should service providers ensure that they can accommodate the specific needs of Travellers who are nomadic, but policies or practices that tend to limit or hinder Traveller nomadism without good reason may actually be counted as unlawful. With this in mind, nomadism can be accommodated by: taking a strategic approach to the provision of Traveller accommodation; ensuring that specific services are adapted so that they are equally accessible to those Travellers who choose to retain a more nomadic way of life (DOE, 1999: 1).

By default, the provisions within the HTAA 1988, the HA 1998 and within the statement of the DOE (1999) suggest that transient sites should have been implemented across the island by service providers. Evidently, evictions within

---

[15] Email communication received on: 04/05/05.
[16] See: the Irish Statute Book website.
[17] Only one of these sites has been deemed adequate by the Irish Traveller Movement to allow for a nomadic lifestyle. Obviously, more are required.

both jurisdictions remain spurious in contrast to recommendations contained within existing legislation in the Republic of Ireland and policy recommendations made by the DOE in Northern Ireland.

As already mentioned, in 2005, the UENIO 2005 was suspended due to protests from interested groups and concerns of the PSNI regarding Section 75 and human rights obligations.   In contrast to the position taken by the government of the Republic of Ireland with regards to human rights, the fact that the terms of the Human Rights Act 1998 was incorporated within the Northern Ireland's legislature in 2000, prior to consideration of the DUENIO 2004 in Northern Ireland is of salience to the following debate.   However, lately, as will be considered below, two key case law decisions concerning Travellers and human rights have probably influenced the Northern Ireland Office to enforce the Unauthorised Encampments (Northern Ireland) Order 2005 as of July 2006.

Rights versus Wrongs

Morris (2001: 41) has suggested that Articles 8.1 and 8.2 of the Human Rights Act have special connotations for Travellers (see also, Clements & Morris, 2001). Article 8.1 states that: 'Everyone has the right to respect for his private and family life, his home and his correspondence'. Therefore, at the very least it could be conceived that evictions invade an individual's right to respect for a home.[18] Article 8.2 lists the limitations on this right stating:

> There shall be no interference by a public authority with the exercise of this right except such as is in accordance with the law and is necessary in a democratic society in the interests of national security, public safety or the economic well-being of the country, for the prevention of disorder or crime, for the protection of health or morals, or for the protection of the rights and freedoms of others.

Subsequently, it could be considered that as a consequence of evictions, public authorities in the Republic of Ireland and Northern Ireland have *interfered* with the exercise of the right to respect for a home.   Interference is also implicated when trailers and caravans are impounded and families are dispersed into temporary accommodation.[19]   Morris also believes that Article 14, prohibition of discrimination is particularly apposite to Irish Travellers and Gypsies prescribing that:

---

[18] The Act does not define what a home is, thus a home could be interpreted as a trailer or caravan.

[19] In general, Traveller families are large, and there may not be room enough for a whole family at a bed and breakfast establishment.

The enjoyment of the rights and freedoms set forth in this Convention shall be secured without discrimination on any ground such as sex, race, colour, language, religion, political or other opinion, national or social origin, association with a national minority, property, birth or other status.

One important issue related to Article 14 is that in a written reply to the Dáil[20] (October 2003) the Minister for Justice McDowell stated that in his opinion: 'Travellers [Irish] do not constitute a distinct group from the population as a whole in terms of race, colour, descent or national or ethnic origin' (Holland, 2003: 4). The stance taken by the government of the Republic of Ireland is in opposition to that taken in Northern Ireland under the Race Relations (Northern Ireland) Order 1997,[21] and, probably, in violation of Article 14 of the Human Rights Act, set out above. The government of the Republic of Ireland's stance had already been sealed in the First National Report by Ireland to the Committee on the Elimination of All Forms of Racial Discrimination prepared during 2003 and set on official record in early 2004 (DJELR, 2004). The government of the Republic of Ireland's position concerning the (non) ethnicity of Travellers was repeated in the second submission made in 2005 (NCCRI, 2004: 2) and at time of writing (June, 2006) remains steadfast. In light of recent key developments concerning human rights and Travellers in two separate decisions in the UK,[22] (especially with regards to Connors) the government of the Republic of Ireland may be wise to reconsider their decision concerning the ethnic status of Irish Travellers.

In 2004, the European Court of Human Rights (ECHR) in Strasbourg found against the UK in the Connors case on grounds of race. In ruling against the United Kingdom in Connors, the court considered 'the vulnerable position of gipsies [sic] as a minority whose way of life member states are positively

---

[20] Irish Government.

[21] Ethnic status is linked to definitions of Travellers and Gypsies within the Race Relations Amendment Act 2000 in the UK. Section 3 of the Human Rights Act (HRA) required that the Race Relations Act 1976 UK be amended so that interpretation may be consistent as far as possible with Convention rights and this occurred in the Race Relations Amendment Act 2000 in the UK. However the Race Relations Act 1976 had applied only to England, Wales and Scotland until 1997 when the Race Relations (Northern Ireland) Order based on the 1976 Act, became law. Gypsies and Irish Travellers are recognised ethnic groups for the purposes of the Race Relations Act (1976), identified as having a shared culture, language and beliefs. Case law established Gypsies as a recognised ethnic group in 1988 (*CRE v Dutton*) and Irish Travellers in England and Wales in August 2000 (*O'Leary v Allied Domecq*) see Commission for Racial Equality web site.

[22] *Connors v United Kingdom* (2004) 40 EHRR 189; *Leeds City Council (Respondents) v. Price and others,* House of Lords, 08/03/06.

obliged to facilitate' (HOL, 2006: 12: 22).[23] In Strasbourg the ECHR concluded that the local authority *had* contravened the human rights of individuals belonging to the Connors Traveller family under Article 8. In the main, the decision reached in Strasbourg was due to the fact that Connors was resident on a legal site. In addition, it was considered that the terms of Connors' license to reside on the site (as opposed to a tenancy agreement) offered no protection against discrimination unlike in the case of non-Traveller residents protected under the terms of the Mobile Homes Act 1983.[24] The decision reached in Strasbourg suggests that the government of the Republic of Ireland would be legally bound to recognise Travellers as an ethnic minority, should Travellers (on a *legal* as opposed to an *illegal* site) ever take a case against them.

Conversely, with regards to illegal occupation of land, in the second key case decision (*Leeds City Council (Respondents) v. Price and others* 08/03/06; HOL, 2006) the House of Lords found that Leeds City Council had *not* transgressed the human rights of Travellers evicted, as they were *illegally* occupying land owned by the council. Indeed, it was found that Leeds City Council had a right above that of the Travellers to take back possession of land that they owned. What is more, Leeds city council won this case even though it had failed to provide adequate accommodation for Travellers as recommended in a range of reports by the British government (ODPM, 2003: a; ODPM 2003: b; ODPM 2005: a; ODPM 2005: b; ODPM 2006: a; ODPM 2006: b; ODPM 2006; c; ODPM 2006: d). In retrospect, it is highly likely that the Leeds case was the catalyst for Minister David Hanson to propose that the UENIO 2005 in Northern Ireland be enacted. Conclusions can be drawn from these two land mark decisions that Travellers may enjoy the protection that human rights legislation confers *only* if they are legally occupying land.

The two cases above demonstrate the conundrum faced by Travellers. It appears that human rights cannot be invoked whilst land is illegally occupied, even though local authorities have failed in their legal obligations to provide

---

[23] Clearly, the refusal of the government of the Republic of Ireland to recognise Irish Travellers as a distinct ethnic minority implies that they are not facilitating the obligations placed upon them and other member states by the European Union.

[24] Until *Connors v United Kingdom* in the UK, Gypsies and Travellers were considered as licensees as opposed to tenants on local authority sites. The same did not apply to non Gypsy Travellers on Mobile home parks who were considered as tenants. As licensees, Gypsies and Travelllers could be evicted for minor transgressions such as pet dogs not being tied up and it was relatively easy for local authorities to secure evictions. Although British law has recently changed to strengthen the rights of Gypsy Travellers on authorised sites, ruling that they be considered as tenants rather than licensees, it remains to be seen if local authorities meet these obligations. See: ODPM reports in reference section at the end of this article.

sites for Travellers in the first instance. Consequently, given sanctioning of recent harsh anti-trespass laws, it is likely that very soon, illegally encamped Travellers will be placed in a worse position across the island of Ireland to that which they were in prior to the introduction of human rights legislation. Clearly, the recent anti-trespass legislation in the Republic of Ireland when conjoined with new anti-trespass law in Northern Ireland creates an unprecedented island wide threat to a nomadic existence.

In consideration of recent developments in the UK outlined above, human rights may not prove to be the panacea anticipated by illegally encamped Travellers to the issues and concerns facing them. As detailed below however, my research identified a profound difference between the responses of police in Northern Ireland and those of police in the Republic of Ireland of Ireland regarding human rights, evictions, and the concerns of Irish Travellers.

Legal Disjunctures

In Northern Ireland, in particular with relevance to control of illegal encampments and evictions under any legislation, the PSNI (2000) have had an obligation towards consideration of human rights since 2000.[25] The fact that unlike in the Republic of Ireland, Irish Travellers are recognised as an ethnic group under the Race Relations (Northern Ireland) Order 1997 was a factor underpinning the reluctance of the PSNI to become involved, without question, in the evictions of illegally encamped Travellers. It remains to be seen now, under sanctioning of anti-trespass law in Northern Ireland, whether or not the PSNI will be able to uphold obligations in consideration of Section 75. The recent key case decision regarding Travellers and human rights on illegal encampments (*Leeds City Council (Respondents) v. Price and others*) appears to suggest that the PSNI *will* become involved in the evictions of illegally encamped Travellers in future.

In the Republic of Ireland, despite the fact that human rights only became law there under the European Convention on Human Rights Act 2003 (taking effect 31/12/03), as far back as 1999, the Garda were reviewing how their actions may or not be compliant with it. The Garda Síochána launched a Human Rights Initiative in October 1999 called 'Policing and Human Rights: Promoting Best Practice' (Garda Síochána, 1999). Here, the Garda *claimed* that one of the aims and objectives of this human rights initiative was: '[t]o identify groups and individuals who may be at risk [of having their human rights

---

[25] The Policing Board has a responsibility by virtue of Section 3 of the Police (NI) Act 2000 to monitor the compliance of the Police Service with the Human Rights Act 1998. See: PSNI, (2000).

violated] and require support' and to '[d]evelop education/training interventions designed to inculcate respect for human rights and personal dignity in all' (Garda Síochána, 1999: 1). However, following the Garda's 1999 concerns to identify groups and individuals at risk of rights violations, as a consequence of the Housing (Miscellaneous Provisions) Act 2002 they became involved in evictions. It can be posited that had an equivalent to Section 75 been introduced in the Republic of Ireland at the same time as it was introduced in Northern Ireland (in 2000) and, had Travellers been recognised as an ethnic minority by the government of the Republic of Ireland, it is doubtful that the Gardai would have been so quick to become involved in the evictions of illegally encamped Travellers.

Another salient issue related to concerns expressed so far is that recently in England, the CRE (2006) stated that '[T]he courts [in England/Wales] have recognised that travelling and living in a caravan are a reflection of Gypsies' and Irish Travellers' cultural heritage, and not simply a choice of lifestyle that can be ignored (CRE, 2006: 13). By default, due to the Race Relations (Northern Ireland) Order 1997, legislation in Northern Ireland must operate proportionally to the findings in England and Wales revealed by the CRE (2006). Consequently, an onus is created on the government of the Republic of Ireland to recognise the rights of Travellers on par with those recognised in Northern Ireland because a commitment by the state of the Republic of Ireland towards recognition of parity of human rights across the island already exists. Following the Good Friday Agreement of 1998 in a speech to Amnesty International, the Taoiseach stated that:[26]

> In recent times, an important focus of successive Governments in the human rights area has been on Northern Ireland. The Good Friday Agreement, which offers so much hope to everyone on this island, represents a major advance in the protection of human rights throughout Ireland. All sides agreed on 10th April, that any new institutional arrangements must be complemented and underpinned by the systematic and effective protection of human rights. Human rights are not solely the preserve of any nationalist or unionist agenda: they apply to all [sic] people of this island. The Irish Government is committed to taking steps to further strengthen the protection of human rights in this jurisdiction (Taoiseach, 1998).

Despite the Taoiseach's demonstrative speech, McVeigh *et. al* (2003) discussed the related dichotomies which remain unresolved. One outstanding issue on the island at present relates to agreement on a Bill of Rights. McVeigh *et. al* (2003) disclose that a right to nomadism has been recognised in the draft Bill of Rights

---

[26] Irish Prime Minister Bertie Ahern.

in Northern Ireland. As the Irish Government committed itself in the Good
Friday Agreement to introduce human rights protection, McVeigh reveals that:

> [b]y implication of this, the right to nomadism recognised in the draft Northern
> Ireland Bill of Rights should be similarly institutionalised in the Republic of
> Ireland. Similar protection for the rights of nomads should also be included in
> the Joint Charter on Rights for the island of Ireland.'(McVeigh *et. al*, 2003: 68).

Given recent landmark developments concerning Travellers and human rights
decisions discussed above in England, it appears improbable that governments
within both jurisdictions on the island of Ireland will respond to calls for a Bill
of Rights and a Joint Charter of rights recognising nomadism across the island.
Nevertheless, the reluctance of state parties to provide for non-nomadic[27] let
alone nomadic Travellers also indicates the unlikelihood that nomadism will
ever be given the official seal of approval.

Conclusion

Essentially, the HMPA 2002 in the Republic of Ireland and the correspondingly
similar UENIO 2005 about to be enacted in Northern Ireland are indicative of
state parties' frustrations with their ability to control illegal encampments. It
has been shown that anti-trespass law has been used in the Republic of Ireland
and that its counterpart has been considered and will, as of July 2006 be
employed in Northern Ireland, despite critic's observations that existing by-laws
are adequate enough to control illegal encampments. It was also indicated that
if state parties hadn't reneged on earlier recommendations concerning provision
of Traveller accommodation, if they had accurately counted the numbers of
Travellers across the island and had assessed the need for transient sites, perhaps
there would have been no need to introduce and to consider strengthened anti-
trespass legislation.

The landmark *Leeds City Council (Respondents) v. Price and others* case
suggests that in future, despite the fact that local authorities have not provided
adequate alternative provision for them, illegally encamped Travellers will *not*
be protected from eviction by human rights law. Alternatively, the outcome of
Connors v the United Kingdom in 2006, implies that the government of the
Republic of Ireland need to concede to the fact that Irish Travellers are indeed a
distinct ethnic minority, in doing so, the human rights of Travellers residing on
legally tolerated/licensed sites would be strengthened. Failure to recognise Irish
Travellers as a distinct ethnic minority is out of sync with polices in Northern

---

[27] Lack of provision for non-nomadic as well as nomadic Travellers is indicated by the lack
of knowledge by state parties concerning the actual Traveller population.

Ireland and elsewhere in the UK and makes the Taoiseach's avowal of a commitment to strengthen the protection of rights across the two jurisdictions appear very hollow indeed.

References

BBC News (2006) 'Travellers angry over camping law,' http://news.bbc.co.uk/2/hi/uk_news/Northernireland/5081290.stm, 15/06/06, (Accessed: 15/06/06).

Clements, L., Morris, R. (2001) 'The Traveller Law Reform Bill, A Brief Guide', The Traveller Law Research Unit, Cardiff Law School, Cardiff http://www.law.cf.ac.uk/tlru/BriefGuide.pdf (Accessed: 06/05/06).

Commission for Racial Equality, *(2006) Common Ground: Equality, good race relations and sites for Gypsies and Irish Travellers, Report of a CRE inquiry in England and Wales,* http://www.cre.gov.uk/commonground_report.pdf, (Accessed: 15/05/06).

Department of the Environment for Northern Ireland, (1999) 'New Policy for Accommodation on Travellers: Report of the PSI Working Group on Travellers': http://www.newtsnni.gov.uk/consultation/recommendations2.htm (Accessed: 12/05/06).

Department of Justice Equality and Law Reform, (2004) *First National Report by Ireland under the UN International Convention on the Elimination of All Forms of Racial Discrimination,* http://www.justice.ie/80256E010039C5AF/vWeb/pcJUSQ5ZDD7C-en, (Accessed: 23/05/06).

Equality Commission for Northern Ireland, (2004) 'Response to the Department of Social Development's Draft Unauthorised Encampments (Northern Ireland) Order 2004,' http://www.equalityni.org/uploads/word/FinCommRespUnauthorisedEncampmentsOrder131204.doc, (Accessed: 07/05/06).

Garda Síochána, 'Human Rights Initiative', (1999), http://www.garda.ie/angarda/col/human.html, (Accessed: 06/05/06).

Holland, K. (2003) 'McDowell criticised for Traveller remark', Irish Times, 17/10/03, p.4.

House of Lords, (2006), Opinions of the Lords of Appeal for Judgement in the Cause Kay and others and another (FC) (Appellants) v. London Borough of Lambeth and others (Respondents), *Leeds City Council (Respondents) v. Price and others* (FC) (Appellants), 08/03/06.

Irish Human Rights Commission, (2005), *Submission of the Irish Human Rights Commission to the United Nations Committee on the Elimination of*

Racial Discrimination in Respect of Ireland's First National Report Under the International Convention for the Elimination of all Forms of Racial Discrimination,
http://www.ihrc.ie/home/default.asp, (Accessed: 12/02/06).

Irish Traveller Movement (2003) 'An Analysis of the use of the Housing (Miscellaneous   Provisions   Act   2002   Forced   Eviction', http://www.itmtrav.com/, (Accessed: 12/05/06).

Joyce, D. (2003) Irish Traveller Movement Traveller Legal Unit Presentation to The Burren Law School; *Outsiders and the Law, Including Those Forced Out by Disability, Ethnicity or Stigma,'* 13/05/03, Newtown Castle, Ballyvaughan, Co. Clare.

McVeigh, R. Donahue,M. Ward,M. (2003), *Misli Crush, Misli, [Cant for go move, shift] Irish Travellers and Nomadism,* A research report for the Irish Traveller Movement and Traveller Movement (Northern Ireland), working paper presented 12/12/03 at Trinity College Dublin, (Final report document: http://www.itmtrav.com/pdf/MISLI-CRUSH-MISLI.pdf, Accessed: 20/05/06).

Morris, R. (2001) 'Gypsies & Travellers: new policies, new approaches' In: *Police Research & Management,* 2001, vol. 5-1 pp. 41-9.

National Consultative Committee on Racism and Interculturalism, (2004) The Importance of Recognising Travellers as an Ethnic Group: Submission to the Joint Oireachtas Committee on Human Rights, Dublin.

NTACC, (2004) *Review of the Operation of the Housing (Traveller Accommodation) Act 1998, Report by the National Traveller Accommodation Consultative Committee to the Minister for Housing and Urban Renewal,* Custom House, Dublin.

Northern Ireland Council for Voluntary Action, (2004)

'NICVA'S Response to Proposal for Control of Unauthorised Encampments,' http://www.nicva.org/uploads/docs/p_UnauthorisedEncampments_200404.p df (Accessed: 05/05/06).

Northern Ireland Human Rights Commission, (2004) 'Response of the Northern Ireland Human Rights Commission to the Draft Unauthorised Encampments (Northern Ireland) Order 2004,'
http://www.nihrc.org/documents/landp/149.doc (Accessed: 07/05/06).

Northern Ireland Housing Executive, (2005: a), District Housing Plan 2005-2006,
http://www.nihe.gov.uk/publications/reports/Dp2005/CraigavonDP2005.pdf. (Accessed: 24/05/06).

—. (2005: b), *Evaluation of Traveller Grouped Housing,* ww.nihe.gov.uk, (Accessed: 19/12/05).

Office of the Deputy Prime Minister, (2003: a), *Local Authority Gypsy/Traveller Sites in England*, by Pat Niner, Crown Copyright, London.

—. (2003: b), *Counting Gypsies and Travellers: A Review of the Gypsy Caravan Count System*, Crown Copyright, London.

—. (2005: a) *Government Response to the ODPM Select Committee's Report on Gypsy and Traveller Sites*, http://www.publications.odpm.gov.uk/pubdetails.asp?pubid=1456Cm, (Accessed: 15/05/06).

—. (2005: b) *Planning Policy Guidance Note 3: Housing Update Planning for Sustainable Communities in Rural Areas*, Crown Copyright, London.

—. (2006: a) *Gypsy and Traveller Accommodation Assessments, Draft Practice Guidance*, Crown Copyright, London.

—. (2006: b), *Planning for Gypsy and Traveller Caravan Sites*, Crown Copyright, London.

—. (2006: c), *Definition of the Term 'Gypsies and Travellers' for the Purposes of the Housing Act 2004*, Crown Copyright, London.

—. (2006: d), *Local authorities and Gypsys' and Travellers' Guide to Responsibilities and Powers*, Gypsy and Traveller Unit, Crown Copyright, London.

Pavee Point Travellers Centre, (2005), R. Fay (ed.), *Irish Travellers Shadow Report: A Response to Ireland's First and Second Report on the International Convention on the Elimination of all forms of Racial discrimination (CERD)* Pavee Point, Dublin.

Police Service of Northern Ireland, (2000), *The Police Service of Northern Ireland Human Rights Programme of Action*, http://www.psni.police.uk/programme_of_action.pdf#xml=http://www.psni. police.uk/scripts/texis.exe/webinator/search/xml.txt?query=Good+Relations +Duty+under+Section+75+&pr=internet&order=r&cq=&id=42eba82f9, (Accessed: 27/07/05).

—. (2003) *Transparency Policy*, http://www.psni.police.uk/transparency_policy_final_amended_30.5_03.doc (Accessed: 27/07/05).

—. (2004) *The Police Service of Northern Ireland Human Rights Programme of Action*, http://www.psni.police.uk/programme_of_action.pdf#xml=http://www.psni. police.uk/scripts/texis.exe/webinator/search/xml.txt?query=Good+Relations +Duty+under+Section+75+&pr=internet&order=r&cq=&id=42eba82f9, (Accessed: 27/07/05).

The Taoiseach, (1998), address by the Taoiseach at the Amnesty International Lunch, 27-11-98, http://www.taoiseach.gov.ie/index.asp?docID=1050, (Accessed: 15/04/06).

Traveller   Visibility   Group,   (2003)   untitled   website   document:
    http://groups.msn.com/TravellerVisibilityGroup/judgeconolearysentencedtw
    otravellers.msnw, (Accessed: 07/05/06).
Unison, (2006) 'Census to reveal true Traveller and minority ethnic group
    numbers',
    http://www.unison.ie/search/frame_search.php3?span=web&words=Census
    %20to%20reveal%20true%20Traveller%20and%20minority%20ethnic%20
    group (Accessed: 21/04/ 06).
UTV, (2006) 'Illegal camps could lead to jail',
    http://u.tv/newsroom/indepth.asp?id=74137&pt=n, (Accessed: 17/06/06).

CHAPTER FIVE

ON THE INTERPRETATION OF A WORD: "PORRAJMOS" AS HOLOCAUST

IAN HANCOCK

Holocaust scholarship came late to the Romanies, and even now, the Romanies who died in Hitler's Europe are usually grouped together in published studies with those referred to as "other non-Jewish" victims: the Poles, the Jehovah's Witnesses, homosexuals and so on. I have always regarded this as a mistaken categorization, if such must be made at all, because I interpret the word *holocaust* to mean the implementation of the "Final Solution" directive, *viz.* genocidal action intended to eradicate entire populations from the sphere of influence of the Third Reich, with the intention of purifying the gene pool of an intended "master race."

There were only two such directives: The Final solution of the Jewish Question and The Final Solution of the Gypsy Question[1]. Not one other targeted group was slated for extermination, nor was the focus of a "final solution." That being the case, this awful chapter in the European Romani experience—an event that has become part of our very anthem *Gelem Gelem*—had to be moved away from the shadow of another people's history, and the first step towards achieving that was to give it a name, and the most widely used word for the Romani Holocaust now is *Porrajmos*.

---

[1] The earliest Nazi document referring to "the introduction of the total solution to the Gypsy problem on either a national or an international level" was drafted under the direction of State Secretary Hans Pfundtner of the Reichs Ministry of the Interior in March, 1936, and the first specific reference to "the final solution of the Gypsy question" was made by Adolf Würth of the Racial Hygiene Research Unit in September, 1937. The first official Party statement to refer to the *endgültige Lösung der Zigeunerfrage* was issued in March, 1938, signed by Himmler; this is reproduced in full in Hancock (2002:38-9).

It has recently been claimed that this is an interpretation of my own invention[2]: it isn't. It was offered as a possible word for "Holocaust" by a Kalderash Romani whose name I regrettably haven't remembered, at an informal lunchtime gathering in the conference centre bar in Snagov in Romania in 1993. A number of us were discussing what to call the Holocaust in Romani. I thought *porrajmos* was particularly appropriate, but have modified it to *Baro Porrajmos* ("*great* devouring") in my own writings since the word alone could be applied to other genocides besides the Holocaust.

Other suggested words for the Holocaust have included (besides *holokausto*) *maripen* which means "killing," *mudaripen* and *murdaripen*, both of which mean "murder," and *samudaripen*, a creation by a linguist which translates as "all" (*sa-*) + "murder," but which violates the rules of Romani morphology.[3] An earlier publication wholly in Romani referred to it metaphorically as the *Berša Bibahtale*, the "unhappy years" (Puxon & Kenrick, 1988).

Porrav- is the Romani word for "devour," and the noun *porrajmos* means "devouring." There is no other word in the language that means "devour" specifically; there is *xa-* "eat," *nakhav-* "swallow" and *parvar-* "feed," but only *porrav-* means "devour," *i.e.* to eat wolfishly. Like *nakhav-*, the basic meaning of which is "make (something) pass," "devour" is the extended application of the basic meaning of the verb *porrav-* which is "open wide." It descends from Old Indo-Aryan *sputa-*, through Middle Indo-Aryan *phuta* "to open up," and its commonest application in the Indo-Aryan languages spoken in India today is to blossoming, as of flowers (Turner, 1966:800).

---

[2] Presumably meaning me, gypsilorist Michael Stewart (2004:564) says "an American Romany intellectual has coined the term Porrajmos, the 'devouring', but one is still more likely to find this term on the internet than on the lips of Roma in the lands occupied by the Germans during the Second World War." Speaking for most of Hungary's nearly one million Romanies he adds "in fact since the term *porrajmos* has also an obscene meaning, it has recently been rejected by most Hungarian Romani speakers who use the calqued term *holocausto*" (*op. cit.,* 578, *n.* 7. But see also Gábor, 2000). As a correction to these assumptions, (a) I'm not American, (b) I didn't invent the word, and (c) *holocausto* (correctly *holokausto* in either Hungarian or Romani orthography) is not a calque but a loanword – a calque is the translation of an idiomatic use, not a direct lexical adoption. Clark and Greenfields (2006:25) have also attributed the word to me: "In the twentieth century anti-Gypsy exclusion came in the extreme form of what Professor Ian Hancock has termed 'O Baro Porrajmos' – the 'Great Devouring' or Gypsy Holocaust – carried out under the Nazis in Germany."

[3] Objecting to a proposed victim-specific word for the Holocaust is not just a Romani issue; a debate over the use of *Shoah* for the Jewish Holocaust and calls for its disuse have recently been ongoing in the French press (Meschonnic, 2005).

The root has survived in a number of Romani dialects with various interpretations, both literal and metaphorical. Thus in Kalderash Vlax it means among other things "open up, rip up, gape, devour, show the teeth, yawn, glare, stare, scream, cheat, pitch a tent" and "stick out the tongue" (Boretzky & Igla, 1994:222, Gjerdman and Ljungberg 1963:322, *et al.*). Demeter & Demeter have only "open wide (the eyes or mouth)" for *porravav* (1990:122; 263), also the only meanings provided by Barthélémy (*n.d.*:116) and Calvet (1993:277). In Bosnian Vlax *poṛav-* means "force open, disjoin, devour, open the eyes, open the mouth," while the noun *poṛavipe* means "an opening"(Uhlik, 1939: *n.p.*). Uhlik's later dictionary, however, has only *nakhavimata* for "devouring" (1983:304) and "rape" as the sole meaning of *poṛavipe* (1983:336). For Macedonian Romani Petrovski & Veličkovcki have *poravipe* "gape" (1998:428). Czech Romani has *našav-* for "devour" and *zgvalcin-* for "rape" (Hübschmannová *et al.*, 1991: 189; 288).

Metaphorically it has the extended meanings as dissimilar as "to rape" and "to bother someone." In Sinti, its derived noun *poravipen* means "a widening or opening up," and by metaphorical extension "freedom" or "access."

In various Vlax dialects, derived verbal and adjectival forms include *porradjov-* "to stretch, widen, extend," *porrado* "spacious," "roomy," "gape-mouthed," "legs astride or akimbo," and "stepping." Derived noun forms as metaphors include *porradi* "vagina" (also with the adjectival meaning of "deflowered"), and *porravipe* "rape."

It is in the sense of "devour," however, that *Porrajmos* was offered. Gjerdman and Ljungberg (*loc. cit.*) give the example *te dikhleasas o sap ke prea xantsi xal, poṛadeasas les atuntši* "if the snake should see that the man ate too little, then he would devour him."

The word has been objected to by some because of some other possible meanings, specifically its use as a euphemism for "rape"[4]. I happen to think this further interpretation, together with "scream" and "gape" and "tear asunder" simply adds to the overall force of the word, for what the Romani genocide did to our people. My own objection, if I had one, would be that in the Sinti dialect it has quite the opposite meaning, and the Sinti Romanies suffered especially harshly in the Nazi genocide.

"Rape" can be expressed in Vlax Romani in a number of other ways; *silov-i-* as a verb, *silovimos* or *sìla* as a noun (*l- pe sìla* "take by force, rape"

---

[4] Romani does not have prefixing except in some dialects heavily influenced by non-Romani syntax, *e.g.* Czech Romani *de-našel*, "flee," English Romani *for-del* "forgive." Like *samudaripen*, the word for "international" (*sathemengo*) is a creation by a non-Romani linguist. The one morpheme usually regarded as an enclitic, viz. *bi* ("without," "un-"), is in fact an independent word, and can be separated from its referent: *bi murro mobìli* "without my car."

with the Slavic word *sila*—also with its Slavic meaning meaning of "force" or "power" in Romani). The more vulgar expression *kurr- pe sìla*, is also heard, both expressions no doubt originating with forced concubinage during the centuries of slavery. In Vlax, *porrav-* can also refer to male sexual arousal.

But these objections from the few lack weight. I'm reminded of the humorous Monty Python "Wankel Rotary Engine" sketch on television many years ago about "suggestive" words and phrases in English. Those who object to *Porrajmos* are either demonstrating the same sort of schoolboy sniggering, or else are objecting purely *in order* to object, which is after all a fundamentally Romani response (although we can expect reaction to the arguments being made here from the non-Romani ethnic police too). The same Romani speakers have no qualms about using such phrases as *xav tj'o kar*, *xav tj'i mindž*, *xav tj'e pele* for "please," and which are not metaphors or euphemisms in any sense. By this reasoning, such common English words as "pussy," "cock," "prick," "tit," "bum," "dick," "ass," and so on should be condemned and replaced by "kitty," "rooster," "pierce," "parus," "tramp," "Ritchie" and "donkey," etc. Some people actually promote this kind of word-avoidance; for marketing purposes rape seed oil is now being sold as "canola oil"— which should particularly please those worried by the word *Porrajmos*.

The same argument would lead us to avoid using the word for "heavy" (*phari*) because it is a common euphemism for "pregnant," and is used to save one from having to utter the real word for this condition (*khamni*); likewise, should we never use the proper word for a fig (*smò□ina*), since it is also a slang word for vagina? It seems that we now need euphemisms for our euphemisms.

Nevertheless use of the word *Porrajmos* is spreading. It turns up in the texts and titles of numerous articles and chapters, a book, and to date it is the name of one documentary film. It has given an identity and a name to the most tragic event in our entire history, and moves it from the collective into the particular. Whether the word will stand the test of time remains to be seen.

Acknowledgements

I want to thank Ronald Lee and Donald Kenrick for their useful comments on this essay.

References

Barthélémy, André, n.d.. *Dictionnaire du Tsigane Kalderash.* n.p.
Boretzky N. and B. Igla, 1994. *Wörterbuch Romani Deutsch Englisch.* Wiesbaden: Harrassowitz.
Calvet, Georges, 1993. *Dictionnaire Tsigane-Français.* Paris: L'Asiathique.

Clark, Colin and Margaret Greenfields, 2006. *Here to Stay: The Gypsies and Travellers of Britain.* Hatfield: The University of Hertfordshire Press.

Demeter, R.S. & P.S. Demeter, 1990. *Gypsy-Russian and Russian-Gypsy Dictionary (Kalderash Dialect).* Moscow: Russky Yazyk.

Gábor Bernáth, ed., 2000. *Porrajmos: E Roma Seron Kon Perdal Zhuvinde – Roma Holocaust Túlélők Emlékeznek.* Budapest: Royal Dutch Embassy.

Gjerdman, O. & Eric Ljungberg, 1963. *The Language of the Swedish Coppersmith Gipsy Johan Dimitri Taikon.* Uppsala: Lundquist.

Hancock, Ian, 2002. *We Are the Romani People.* Hatfield: The University of Hertfordshire Press.

Hübschmannová, M., Hana Šebková & Anna Žigová, 1991. *Romsko-Český a Česko-Romský Slovník.* Prague: SPN.

Meschonnic, Henri, 2005. "Pour en finir avec le mot «Shoah»," *Le Monde*, Feb. 20th. Petrovski, T. & B. Veličkovcki, 1998. *Makedonsko-Romski i Romsko-Makedonski Rečnik.* Skopje: Vorldbuk.

Puxon, Grattan & Donald Kenrick, 1988. *Berša Bibahtale.* London: Romanestan Publications.

Stewart, Michael, 2004. "Remembering without commemoration: the mnemonics and politics of Holocaust memories among European Roma," *Journal of the Royal Anthropological Institute*, n.s., 10:561-582.

Turner, Ralph, 1966. *A Comparative Dictionary of the Indo-Aryan Languages.* London: Oxford University Press.

Uhlik, Rade, 1939. [*A Bosnian Romani Dictionary*], *ms.* Edited and translated into English by Frederick George Ackerly, *Journal of the Gypsy Lore Society*, 1941-3.

Uhlik, Rade, 1983. *Srpskohrvatsko-Romsko-Engelski Rečnik.* Sarajevo: Svjetlost.

CHAPTER SIX

COMBATING SOCIAL EXCLUSION IN IRELAND: SOCIAL CAPITAL AND THE WORK OF THE CORK TRAVELLER WOMEN'S NETWORK

LOUISE HARRINGTON,
CORK TRAVELLER WOMEN'S NETWORK

AND MICHAEL HAYES,
UNIVERSITY OF LIMERICK TRAVELLER AND ROMA INITIATIVE

In this essay we examine some aspects of a unique project which occurred amongst an urban community on the north side of Cork city recently. This project known as the *Barrel-Top Wagon Project* explored the potential of the Community Arts to contribute to issues of cultural recognition and democracy and to act as a catalyst for the generation of social capital. The project involved a case study as undertaken amongst and in collaboration with a group of Irish Travelling people from across Cork city, in the south-west of Ireland. Within the past two years, Irish society has begun to examine the role of "social capital" as a contributory element to the country's economic development but also as regards its potential for the enrichment of Irish social and cultural reproduction. It is arguable that the past decade has witnessed an undue emphasis on Ireland's social capital in purely economic terms – the term "benchmarking" is a commonly-issued mantra in present-day Irish (and European) discourse for instance - an emphasis which is by definition overly-narrow and limiting. Ireland is one of the world's biggest exporters of software for example – a field which frequently demands a level of creativity and innovation on a par with any artistic work and a field which has acted to buttress much of Ireland's economic recovery to date. In this essay we argue that the term "social capital" ought to be perceived as having a wider and more inclusive remit. Social capital, we argue, is not simply a type of unit-based yardstick with which to define and measure economic production. It has a more all-encompassing and holistic function than this. In reality social capital should stand for any individual or group of individuals who have the capability to make a life that is fulfilling for themselves and enriches their community. Community arts and the recollection and representation of a minority group's culture and life experience such as was undertaken in Cork's Barrel-Top Wagon Project also works to create social capital through integrating all of the intelligences and thereby bolstering people's social and cultural awareness. It is particularly beneficial for young people from minority groups such as the Irish Travellers, many of whom have been marginalised and alienated from the social and cultural processes of the "majority" or non-Traveller community. Projects like the Barrel-Top Wagon Project enable the younger generation of Travellers to become self-reliant and confident of their own abilities and attributes as Irish citizens in a state increasingly characterised by a multiculturalism which incorporates a multiplicity of different cultural and linguistic groups. While social capital does not solve social problems, injustices and inequalities it nevertheless provides people with the skills and the capabilities that make it possible for these ills to be eliminated.

Traveller Arts

This Traveller arts project was one of the first studies ever undertaken in Ireland by that minority known as the Irish Travellers where members of the Traveller community interrogated the potential of the community arts to generate a powerful cultural statement about their own community, a community and a culture which has consistently suffered a lack of any worthwhile recognition in its country of origin. The fact that this arts project was judged very successful by commentators both within the Traveller community itself and within the wider Irish public or "settled community" and was the subject of a number of documentaries and significant media attention highlights the potential that such a form of social capital has for the development of networks on both the individual and community level. To underline why this project was unique and the subject of commentary within the mainstream Irish media it is necessary to state a few simple facts, some "bald" realities which are common knowledge amongst activists and development workers (both Travellers and settled community members) who work in conjunction with the Irish Travellers on a day-to-day basis, but which, strange as it may seem, would come as a surprise to many people not associated with development work or the Traveller community in Ireland. The present-day circumstances of Irish Travellers were the context and the catalyst for the Barrel Top Wagon Project's inception. These circumstances, include a long history of Traveller "othering" by the non-Traveller community in Ireland and are relatively unique in a Western European sense. A long-established minority whose history in recent generations has been primarily a non-literate one, the Irish Travellers – (who are today increasingly ascribed the rubric of an ethnic minority in Irish media discourse) - have traditionally lived very much on the margins of "mainstream" Irish society and have been the object of a particular and virulent form of social exclusion. Official figures estimate that there are about 28,000 Travellers living in the Republic of Ireland with a further 1500 in Northern Ireland, although there are many development workers, activists and Travellers who would argue that the numbers are probably higher than this, particularly if "mixed" families where one parent is a member of either the Traveller or the settled community are considered part of the equation. The past few decades have seen a substantial deterioration in the relationship between the Traveller community and the "settled" community as officially represented in the form of local authorities. The reasons for this deterioration in social relations are wide-ranging and an essay as brief as this would not do justice s to a correct analysis of their complexity. Suffice to say that the reasons for increased tension between the Travelling and the settled communities have to do with struggles in relation to class, changes in economic relations between the Traveller and settled communities, the thorny issue of land use in an increasingly urbanised country and the increased attempts on the part of the State to intervene in what is often defined as the Traveller "problem" [1]. It is no small irony that the arrival of immigrants to Ireland, including Roma (Gypsies) from the former Eastern bloc, has recently pushed the question of interculturalism and the multicultural nature of Irish society to the fore in a way which never occurred previously. Recent tensions between the Traveller and settled communities do not disguise the fact, however, that there has been a long history of anti-Traveller prejudice, often termed racism, in Ireland. This question of ant-Traveller racism is a pervasive theme in the literature on Travellers. Prejudice against Travellers is entrenched in Irish society. They have a pariah status (Gmelch, 1977); they live in "caste-like isolation" (McCarthy 1971, 1). McGréil's research into Irish prejudice

---

[1] In October 2004, for example, there was a largescale protest from the Traveller community and Traveller activist organisations such as Pavee Point at a large halting site in Finglas, north Dublin. The protest was a response to the erection of a concrete barrier at the entrance to the halting site by the local authorities who alleged that anti-social behaviour was prevalent in that area. Families living in the area were also searched in a dawn raid on the sight by armed police who were searching for evidence of weapons and stolen goods which they alleged were being used by a criminal element. The barrier forced Traveller families living on the site having to travel many miles in a circuitous route to get in and out of the halting site and to take their children to local schools and shops. After a series of protests and a mediation process between the Travellers and local authorities it was agreed to remove the barrier.

(1977, 1996) chronicles a substantial deterioration in attitudes towards Travellers since the early 1970s, with the consequence that Travellers are often treated as a "lower caste" in society (1996).

Many recent writers have described the discrimination affecting Travellers as a form of racism. (O'Connell, 1992a; 2002 Acton; Okely, Ní Shúinéar, McDonagh and others in McCann et al, 1994; McLoughlin, 1995; McVeigh, 1992a, 1992b, 1996, 1997). This racism has been addressed by Traveller organizations like the Irish Traveller Movement, Pavee Point and anti-racist organizations such as Harmony. It is arguable however that the issue of anti-Traveller racism has only been addressed primarily in two contexts. One context is that of explaining that a minority ethnic group such as Travellers experience racism. Another is the detailing of the different forms of racism that have been experienced by Travellers. This emphasis on advocacy has meant that the issue of why anti-Traveller racism happens has remained relatively under-theorised[2] by both academic commentators and development activists. There are a number of possible explanations for this. The fact that Ireland was a British colonial outpost for many centuries meant that many English State historians and commentators rarely distinguished between Travellers as a specific social and cultural category within the mass of the, often mobile, Irish poor. The few social records which have survived and which do include references to Travellers are not virtually all from the hands of non-Travellers and therefore needed to be treated with caution. The fact that, as already outlined, Travellers make up only a tiny minority within the Irish population as a whole – i.e. less than 1% of the population may also provide a certain explanation as to their invisibility in the historical record. What is abundantly clear from most references to Travellers, both current and historic, however, is the fact that Travellers have for many decades been translated into a dramatic spectacle of cultural Otherness. Frequently they have been described using a series of discursive strategies and popular stereotypes and incorporating an array of suspicions and superstitions. These same reductionist stereotypes have been the subject of constant re-

---

[2] Acton (1994) has highlighted the inherent racism in the very nature of scholarly enquiry into the perceived distinctions between different groupings of Gypsies and Travellers. He argues that academic attempts to locate distinctions between different groups originate in a denial of the realities of slavery and genocide as inflicted on Gypsies/Travellers in both the sixteenth and twentieth centuries. He advises those interrogating the ascriptions by which nomadic people define themselves to remember the importance of understanding the nature and context of such definitions, and their fluidity, as and when imposed by Gypsies/Travellers themselves. What Gypsies/Travellers are doing when they refer to themselves as one and not the other may depend on the context in which they find themselves and the dangers or opportunities inherent in such situations.

articulation in Ireland over recent centuries and have been used to justify Travellers' exclusion from "regular" society. They have also been used to support the majority society's view that to solve the Traveller issue, it is necessary that Travellers be assimilated and their nomadic culture, an apparent anachronism in the modern nation-state, outlawed.

One of the most powerful forces the modern nation-state has had in its "battle" against Travellers and other minorities is the power of definition, representation and the power of the written word in particular. This is an area which is of particular significance in the current climate given the claims for ethnic status being pursued by some Traveller activists and activist groups in Ireland. Because Traveller culture has primarily been non-literate, how their culture is defined is frequently beyond the control of Travellers themselves. Travellers are at a disadvantage when attempting to negotiate their struggle for identity and recognition in a society which is increasingly state-oriented and where the power of the media and the presentation of "image" is paramount. Travellers themselves have scarcely been able to exercise any influence on the way in which their identity has been constructed over the past century or so. Indeed it is the case that the Traveller image, as defined by non-Travellers has become institutionalized in Ireland in the same way that the image of the Roma (Gypsy) people, part-negative and part-romantic has become so institutionalized in Western tradition that it has become part of the Western cultural heritage. The survival of Traveller culture, while depending primarily on the powers of the Travelling community to withstand the forces of assimilation and acculturation to the majority society, is also largely dependent on the attitude of the majority or non-Traveller society to this minority culture. It is this reality that lay at the kernel of the particular aims and hopes of those Travellers who initiated the Barrel-Top Wagon Project. It was felt that by "putting the culture out there" it would be possible to create a respect and recognition for Traveller culture that has not been there to date. The fact that this project incorporated a strong oral history remit as recorded by Travellers themselves and was funded as part of the Cork 2005 Capital of Culture celebrations served only to add a further incentive for the Project's success.

Ireland, Social Capital and Social Change

It is only very recently that Irish society and its organs of state have begun to examine the role of "social capital", not only as a contributory element in the country's economic development but also as regards its potential for the enrichment of Irish social and cultural reproduction generally. During the past year, a concern with the question of social capital, and the lack thereof, has even been expressed at the highest levels of government. Indeed the current Irish Taoiseach (Prime Minister) Bertie Ahern used a keynote speech[3] marking the nineteenth anniversary of the Ireland's (1916) Easter Rising, the rebellion which consolidated the independence of the Irish republic to call for "a new culture of active citizenship" in Irish society. That the leader of the Irish government should feel the need to make such a plea is indicative of the speed with which Irish society has changed within the space of a decade. A period of economic "boom", often referred to as the "Celtic Tiger" years has reversed decades of severe poverty and helped Ireland to surpass many of its European neighbours in terms of economic prosperity. The speed with which change has occurred in Ireland both economically and socially however has left people reeling. Irish people who emigrated a decade or more ago frequently confess to finding present-day Ireland unrecognisable when compared with the old Ireland of mass emigration and unemployment which they were forced to leave. Recent prosperity has brought with it a new set of controversies and questions, however, questions with which Irish society has had "teething problems". Poor infra-structure in terms of roads and health services when combined with a huge growth in urban sprawl in larger cities such as Dublin has meant longer commuter times, gridlock, soaring house prices, long queues in hospitals for the most routine services and the necessity for most young couples that they both work in order to meet mortgage repayments. It is also the case that approximately half a million people, many of them from the former Eastern Bloc, have immigrated to Ireland within the past few years as a response to the improved employment prospects in Ireland. When all of these factors are taken into consideration it is unsurprising that forms of "social capital" previously taken for granted in Ireland have begun to suffer. Many parents find that they have little time to spend with their children while the numbers volunteering for charity work, social and sports clubs and other voluntary forms of community involvement have gone into a steep decline. Unfortunatley, the very swift and wide-ranging nature of this profound social change also holds within it the potential to exacerbate the "othering" or social exclusion of minority groups such as the Irish Travellers and hamper their efforts to improve their position within Irish society. What way the wheel turns depends very much on the steps being taken by the Irish public and, indeed, the Irish state, to make Ireland a more inclusive country in which to live in the short to medium-term.

To examine the consequences of these emerging factors as regards social cohesion the Irish government set up a task force last year (2005) to examine the question of active citizenship on the part of Irish people. Leading experts on the

---

[3] "Taoiseach calls on citizens to do more for society", *The Irish Times*, 10/4/06.

subjects of social cohesion and social capital have also been invited to Ireland in recent times including American social thinker Robert Putnam who addressed the concept of social capital in a speech[4] given to OECD education ministers in Dublin not so long ago. It is within such a context, one which encompasses far-reaching social change, that we provide some brief observations on the importance of social capital to the social cohesion of Irish society as a whole and more particularly on the local level as applied to minorities such as the Irish Traveller community.

Social Capital and Social Cohesion?

None of the aims outlined in our introduction to the Barrel-Top Wagon Project could have been explored adequately without this initial and thorough discussion of the value of the "elusive" concept that is "social capital" itself, a discussion which took place at the very initial stages of the Project. Social capital is evident when people take up their pens to write a book or take to the stage as musicians or actors. It is the result of that special conjunction that occurs between the artist and their creative activity as it resonates within the minds of listener and audience. A strong argument can be made that the past decade has witnessed an over-emphasis on Ireland's social capital in purely economic terms to the detriment of its other aspects. Cognisant of this fact a strong effort was made at the beginning of this Project to analyse "social capital" in terms of the Traveller-settled matrix in Cork city as something which had a wider and more inclusive remit, a holistic remit which could enrich two communities whose social and intra-community relationships have undoubtedly been strained and tense at various periods in the not-to-distant past.

The research that bulwarked the Barreltop Wagon Project was therefore foregrounded within a framework incorporating the values of emancipatory practice. A particular focus of the project was on the non-recognition of Traveller culture in Ireland as a form of oppression and the consequent exploration of the community arts as a potential emancipatory strategy with which to combat this. The focal point for the project was therefore on the collation of Travellers' subjective testimonies regarding their experiences of oppression and the impact which the Barrel Top Wagon Project had both on the personal and political level. To date campaigns for cultural democracy have been based on the premise that society harbours major inequalities in how the values and meanings of different groups are recognised and reproduced in the dominant culture (Williams, 1968) and that this perpetuates other forms of

---

[4] See Website: www.ksg.harvard.edu/saguaro/

oppression and domination. Advocates of cultural democracy have frequently called for broader access to the expression and recognition of cultural values and heritage (McGonagle, 2001). Both Taylor (1994) and Honneth (2003) have highlighted cultural recognition as a paramount and fundamental citizenship right, one which is implicitly linked to the potential for full participation in society and one which is generally manifested in both the ideological and structural realms.

Recognition claims can include a range of strategies including the specific legal protection for members of minority communities from discrimination[5] the protection of the rights of minorities to practice their culture, or active support for the cultural reproduction of minorities and their cultural values (Honneth, 2003). Community arts, as engaged with in the Barrel-Top Wagon Project is one movement amongst many which has challenged the traditional restriction of participation in the arts to a tiny minority of the population. It aims to democratise access to both participation in and consumption of culture.

CAFÉ (1994) – [Community Arts Resource/Training, Dublin] defines community arts as representing a range of collective, creative activities, which emphasise process as well as product and are rooted in communities, reflecting their experiences and working for their benefit. Cultural theorists such as Orton (1997) have highlighted the potential for community arts to engage with issues of voice and contribute to the recognition of marginalized groups. In reality, however, community arts, until recently, have tended to focus primarily on broadening access to artistic production a fact highlighted by McGonagle (2001) who has been critical of recent community arts developments and their tendency to remain solely for the consumption of the communities which produce them. This reality has potentially limited the contribution of the community arts to cultural democracy as evidenced within the Irish and European context to date. Cognisant of this fact, a central feature of the research approach adopted by the Barrel Top Wagon Project was an attempt to engage with "community arts" in terms which implied a democratisation process, one where-by culture as art functions to confer recognition and validation of a minority culture or way of life, a recognition which would be advanced on the wider societal level.

---

[5] The Employment Equality Act (1998) and the Equal Status Act (2000) outlaw discrimination in employment, vocational training, advertising, collective agreements, the provision of goods and services and other opportunities to which the public generally have access on nine distinct grounds. These are: "gender; marital status; family status; age; disability; race; sexual orientation; religious belief; and membership of the Traveller Community." It is important to note however that Irish Travellers are not considered an ethnic minority in the Republic of Ireland; neither are any provisions made for them under the term of 'race.'" - http://www.equality.ie/

Advocates of culture as a form of political action have drawn attention to its normative dimension and its role as a carrier of ideology and discourse in society (Duncombe, 2002). This reality was all too apparent to the participants in this Project, whether Traveller or settled from the Project's earliest stages. Societal validation and recognition is not something which can ever be taken for granted. As this project made clear, it is a reality which constantly needs to be fought for in an arena where culture is itself a site of contestation, power and politics. We hope to examine some of the Barrel-Top Wagon Project's ramifications in terms of minority cultural recognition for the Traveller community in a future essay. We close this essay with a number of these insights as described by Traveller themselves:

> the wagon project is about taking ownership of who we are and where we came from.
> —Mary

> I suppose it brought a lot of them back to realise what their culture was, a lot of them that doesn't understand it....[and helped] Travellers feel proud of their heritage
> —John

> I learned that everything is not lost, there is still hope there like for the Travelling culture, that the culture can still be kept alive. The wagon showed us that, so I hope for the future we will see more [culture projects] and that more people get involved in it. I didn't think that young people could kind of look at it as a cultural thing, you know. And they did and they were very proud of it, so I am hoping there will be more of it, because it would revive the hope in the Travellers that all is not gone, that's what they want
> —Katie

> Before in school the atmosphere was very clingy, because I didn't know about them and they obviously didn't know about me, because I wasn't admitting to it anyway. No matter how hard they tried, they wouldn't get me to admit that I was a Traveller...I used to be ashamed, never, never in my life would I talk Cant and say "feen" or "beoir" or "buffers"...[I thought the others would think] oh you're a Traveller, I don't want to be with you no more...and I'd be left alone
> —Amanda

References

CAFÉ, (1994) *Art & The Community Conference Report*, CAFÉ, Dublin
Foucault, M. (1980) *Power / Knowledge: Selected Interviews and Other Writings* 1972 –1977, London, Harvester Press

Fraser, N. *(2003) Social Justice in the Age of Identity Politics in Fraser, N. &*
Honneth, A. (eds) Recognition or Redistribution, *Verso, London*
Freire, P. (1973) *Pedagogy of the Oppressed,* Penguin, London
Government of Ireland (1983*) Report of the Travelling People Review Body*,
Stationary Office, Dublin
—. (2000) *Equal Status Act (2) 1 –*
http://www.irishstatutebook.ie/ZZA8Y2000S2.html accessed June 2005
—. (1995), *Task Force on the Travelling Community,* Stationary Office, Dublin
Gramsci, A. (1971) Selections from the Prison Notebooks, Exceprt in
Duncombe, S, (2002) (ed) *Cultural Resistance Reader*, Verso, London
Honneth, A. *(2003) Redistribution as Recognition* in Fraser, N. & Honneth, A.
(2003) *Redistribution or Recognition;* Verso, London
Humphries, B. Mertens, D.M. & Truman, C. (2000) *Arguments for an*
"emancipatory" Research Paradigm in Truman, C. Mertens, D.M &
Humphries (eds) Research and Inequality, *UCL Press, London*
Irish Traveller Movement (2002), *Submission to the Development of the*
National Action Plan Against Racism, Irish Traveller Movement, Dublin
MacGréil, M. (1996) *Prejudice in Ireland Revisited*, The Survey & Research
Unit, St Patrick's College, Maynooth
McCann, M., O'Siochain, S, & Ruane, J. (1994) *Irish Travellers Culture and*
Ethnicity Queens University, Belfast
McDonagh, M. (1994) Nomadism in Irish Travellers Identity in McCann, M.,
O'Siochain, S., & Ruane, J. (eds) *Irish Travellers Culture and Ethnicity*
Queens University Belfast
McGonagle, D. (2001) *Community Arts, The Next Five Years Conference*
Report, CAFÉ, Dublin
Moore, J. (1997) *Poverty, Access and Participation in the Arts*, CPA, Dublin
Orton, B. (1997) Community Arts: Reconnecting with the radical Tradition in
Cooke, I. & Shaw, M. (eds) *Radical Community work*, Moray House
Publications, Trowbridge
Williams, R. (1958) *Culture is Ordinary in Gable, R (1989) (Ed)* Resources of
Hope, Culture Democracy and Socialism *Verso, London*
—. (1968) *The idea of a Common Culture,* Exert in Gable, R (1989) (ed)
Resources of Hope, Culture Democracy and Socialism *Verso, London*

CHAPTER SEVEN

SPEAKING THE TRAVELLERS' LIFEWORLD: INSIGHTS FROM JÜRGEN HABERMAS

DAVID O'DONNELL

Only the communicative model of action presupposes language as a medium of uncurtailed communication whereby speakers and hearers, out of the context of their preinterpreted lifeworld, refer simultaneously to things in the objective, social and subjective worlds in order to negotiate common definitions of the situation.
—Jürgen Habermas 1984: 95

Introduction

In this chapter, I draw explicitly on the structural components of a Habermasian lifeworld in order to identify some dynamic processes through which a specific "context" may be theoretically positioned in terms of theory, method, language and situated practice. As Habermas (1996, p. x) himself puts it in Between Facts and Norms:

The basic assumptions of the theory of communicative action (...) branch out into various universes of discourse, where they must prove their mettle in the contexts of debate they happen to encounter.

According to Max Weber, social orders can only be maintained over time as legitimate orders; such orders require more than habit, custom, convention or attitude—legitimate orders rest on a value consensus to the extent that the ideas or values incorporated in such social orders must be intersubjectively recognised (Habermas, 1996). Such intersubjective recognition is achieved mainly through language. The lifeworld-in-system perspective briefly outlined here seems particularly applicable to the emphasis in this collection on the hidden languages of various Traveller lifeworlds and how such languages both constitute and legitimise the social order of "Travellers". Using Habermas' structural components, I outline the importance of each, with an emphasis on such hidden languages as the nexus encompassing Traveller history, culture, tradition and, perhaps most importantly, identity.

Traveller Lifeworld-in-System

At a very broad level, Habermas (1984; 1987a,b; 1994) conceptualises developed economy and society as three basic sub-systems: Money, Power and Lifeworld. The instrumental means-end logics of the systems of both money and power are geared to success, efficiency, control, profit, growth or market share; in contrast, the communicative logic of the human lifeworld is geared to understanding and agreement. This distinction between goal-oriented instrumental action and communicative action is a core distinction at the foundation of Habermasian social theory and social philosophy. Habermas' theory of communicative action (1984, 1987a) allows both System and Lifeworld perspectives to be included in any analysis. Members of a social collective, such as a Traveller community, normally share a largely intangible and tacit lifeworld that only exists in a "uniquely pre-reflexive form of background assumptions, background receptivities or background relations" (Honneth et al., 1981: 16). Such background lifeworlds are to be conceived, according to Habermas (1987a: 124), as "culturally transmitted and linguistically organised stock(s) of interpretative patterns".

Cant, 'the gammon' and other hidden languages can be viewed as constructed from such a tradition. Lifeworlds exist in the plural; within the Traveller 'world' there are many lifeworlds. Habermas (1987a), following Parsons' ideas on culture, society and personality, provides us with broad theoretical guidelines that can be applied in conceptualising Traveller lifeworlds (Figure I). The boundary between System (money; power) and Traveller Lifeworld is, however, not a clear-cut one—these must interpenetrate and reciprocally influence each other—and it is at these seams between systems and Traveller lifeworlds that one often meets tension, contentiousness, mis-understanding, non-communication and at different times and places—hostility and downright warfare. Hence the question: How does the Traveller lifeworld speak?

Figure 1. Contours of a Traveller Lifeworld-in-System

Reproduction Processes	Structural components			Evaluation Dimension
	Traveller Culture	Traveller Community	Traveller Selves	
Cultural Reproduction	1.1 Interpretative schemata fit for consensus: valid processes of knowing [loss of meaning]	1.2 Legitimations [withdrawal of legitimation]	1.3 Behaviour patterns effective in learning & development [crisis in orientation & development]	Rationality of Knowledge
Social Integration	2.1 Obligations [unsettling of collective identity]	2.2 Legitimately ordered interpersonal relations [anomie]	2.3 Social memberships & ownership [alienation]	Solidarity of Members
Socialisation	3.1 Interpretative accomplishments [rupture of tradition]	3.2 Motivations for actions that conform to norms [withdrawal of motivation]	3.3 Interpretative capabilities and personal identities [psycho-pathologies]	Personal Responsibility

Source: adapted from O'Donnell & Henriksen (2002: 95) and Habermas (1987a: 142-3).

The structural components of particular Traveller lifeworlds (culture, community, selves) meet their corresponding needs (cultural reproduction, social integration, socialisation and selves-development) through three dimensions along which communicative action is conducted (reaching understanding, coordinating interaction, effecting socialisation) which in turn are rooted in the structural components of ordinary everyday language and communications (O'Donnell, 1999, 2004), including Cant and other hidden languages. Such a framework is particularly suited to interpretive or ethnographic research and particularly to co-creation work (Henriksen et al., 2004) which specifically demands that Travellers themselves take part in, contribute to and take joint responsibility for findings, conclusions, recommendations, policy initiatives and so on. These identities and interpretative abilities allow for social memberships to form, which, in turn help to mould the interests, behaviour patterns and development goals of particular Traveller groups. Behaviours and future goals evolve from these identities and social memberships that are initially learned through communicative dialogue (O'Donnell and Porter, 2002).

Within their own cultures Travellers negotiate norms of behaviour, agree on boundaries for pursuing personal preferences as well as having some consideration for each other's needs. These norms eventually become part of tacitly taken-for-granted social contracts that guide behavioural processes within Traveller communities. To take just one example; here is Geraldine talking about her experience of not attending secondary school in Ireland and agreeing with her mother on the underlying reasons for not participating in formal second level education:

> ... I think that she [my mother] is right. Young ones who go to secondary school change into something that they're not. They're acting like country people. They're dressing like country people. They don't like jewellery no more. They don't like being a Traveller no more. They don't change in a good way. They're trying to be something that they're not. The point I'm making—the way you go in is the way you should come out with plenty of education but still proud to be a Traveller.
> —Trainees of St. Josephs Training Centre, 2000: 161

We observe here the "fear among some Travellers that formal education educates Traveller children 'out off' their own culture. In some ways formal education is seen to work contrary to, rather than in harmony with, Traveller values and culture" (McDonagh, 2000: 151-2). Let us look at how Winnie McDonagh uses the commonplace word 'formal' here. As Ludwig Wittgenstein, the philosopher of language, puts it:

> One cannot guess how a word functions. One has to look at its use and learn from that. But the difficulty is to remove the prejudice which stands in the way of doing this. It is not a stupid prejudice.
> (2001/1953: § 340, emphasis in original)

For 'formal' here one can read 'System' in Habermas' terms, but this is the system of the dominant Other constructed by and for the 'country' or 'settled' people—where this Other is perceived to colonise the values, norms or traditions of the Traveller lifeworld then it is perceived as a real threat as it will lead to negative consequences as in the areas noted in brackets in Figure I above such as 'unsettling of collective identities' [2.1], 'alienation' [2.3], 'rupture of tradition' [3.1], forms of 'psychopathology' [3.3], and so on. We witness here a clash of different 'forms of life' (Wittgenstein, 2001) with contrasting lifeworld logics, values and norms where the legitimate order of one is perceived, if perceived at all, as illegitimate or alien by the other. Hence the centrality of language in maintaining legitimate Traveller identities within various Traveller lifeworlds. I must welcome here as positive the inclusion recently of a short module on Cant within the Irish primary school curriculum. Recognition of the Other's unique language by Another demands a simultaneous recognition of the uniqueness of the Other.

Situating Traveller culture, Traveller community, and Traveller selves or self-identities within a Habermasian lifeworld (Figure I), which is constituted by and through everyday language, is central to the simple argument that I present here. Such Traveller identity is held together, and regenerated, through the medium of communicative action in Travellers' own everyday language. In the next section I go a little deeper into this key concept of communicative action.

Communicative action

Lifeworlds are held together and regenerated through the medium of what Habermas terms "communicative action" (1984: 86):

> Communicative action refers to the interaction of at least two subjects capable of speech and action who establish interpersonal relations (whether by verbal or extra-verbal means). The actors seek to reach an understanding about the action situation and their plans of action in order to coordinate their actions by way of agreement. The central concept of interpretation refers in the first instance to negotiating definitions of the situation [that] admit of consensus.

The ability to raise "validity claims" within this communicative relation is central to the theory of communicative action (O'Donnell, 2004). I argue strongly here that validity claims are also central to the effective functioning of critical dialogue within Traveller lifeworlds and, perhaps more importantly, in effective functioning of critical dialogue between Traveller and settled 'forms of life'. This latter form of dialogue is both sorely lacking, with exceptions, and yet urgently demanded if Traveller forms of life are to be mutually perceived as legitimate by both Travellers and settled people whether in Ireland, Britain, United States or elsewhere. When two people communicate with each other, face-to-face, body-language or ICT mediated, each utterance that alter makes can be implicitly or explicitly accepted or challenged by ego on a simple "Yes" or "No" basis. Alter is seen as making a claim to validity with each utterance and ego can either accept or reject this claim.

The first, and general, validity claim relates to comprehensibility. In most cases this is simply understood, un-spoken and taken-for-granted; this is not always so, however, at the seams between Traveller lifeworlds and settled systems. One of the original uses of Cant, for example, was to exclude the stranger in conversation, similar to the Gaelic asides of Irish labourers in Britain over the decades. But even when both speak an apparent universal language, such as English, the perceived meanings and 'uses' are often not the same—as in the example of 'formal' education noted above. Comprehensibility, therefore, is not to be simply assumed.

Validity claims of propositional truth and/or efficacy relate to the objective world of facts and/or states of affairs; for example if alter states that the area of a triangle is one third of the base multiplied by the height, ego can reject this claim explicitly with a "No" and provide evidence that the area of a triangle is one half the base multiplied by the height; in terms of states of affairs, a school inspector might state that the new primary school curriculum is working superbly—a Traveller representative on the school board of management may explicitly refuse to accept the validity of this statement, seek further evidence from others around the board table, or produce her own evidence to show that the cultural norms on which the formal system is based in particular curricular areas conflict with the values, norms and attitudes that her own community considers to be appropriate; hence, from her perspective the so-called formal system is not working superbly and is the subject of some unease within her own community.

The validity claim of normative rightness relates to the social world "around here"—what is generally considered normative, socially acceptable and usually "taken for granted" behaviour. For example, a new family moves into a local halting site and after some time the head of this family intimates to the other members that as he is the senior person present he should set the agenda on the type of business to be conducted locally—only to be politely informed that "you can't pull rank on us like that around here!—this is our community, not yours!", that is, the validity of this particular Traveller's actions are not accepted by the other families as they do not conform to the traditional norms of this particular Traveller community.

The validity claim of sincerity/authenticity relates to the (inter)subjective world and is often accepted or rejected implicitly and silently by ego who decides whether alter is being genuine, sincere or authentic. When rejected explicitly, one may hear such comments as – "Pull the other one!", "D'you think I came down in the last shower—or What!", and so on.

What is distinctive about these validity claims is that thinking about them in the overall context of a Habermasian lifeworld may provide one with insight into both the depth and quality of the communicative interactions within a Traveller community, and in the dialogue between settled and Traveller communities. In the latter case, where such validity claims exist the possibility of constructive dialogues and consequent constructive actions is possible—without them cooperative agreement is almost impossible to achieve.

As the brief discussion on validity claims above is designed to demonstrate, communicative action is a fragile process and when this process is endangered by system influences (such as the dominance of English language and media; the intrusion of formal educational logics; one way interventions from the all-knowing powers on high; and so on), Traveller lifeworlds suffer. By implication, anything that negatively influences the ability to raise these validity claims will reduce, or perhaps even destroy, the legitimate functioning of Traveller communities—most centrally, the loss of language and the consequent loss of identity.

Using Habermas' dimensions of evaluation, one can seek to identify areas where systemic influences colonise or destroy effective and legitimate aspects of particular Traveller communities leading to experiences such as loss of meaning, anomie, various forms of alienation, rupturing of traditions and the unsettling of collective identities (see Figure I)—in other words, to influences that prevent Traveller communities from maintaining their sense of identity within the broader society, or perhaps destroy them completely. Conversely, one can identify the positive, the empowering, the vibrant, the independent, the confident and the aesthetically enriching. Drawing on some of the fundamental points of Habermas' massive oeuvre, I have briefly presented here a social theoretical map within which Travellers, researchers, policy makers and others can begin to think substantively about the language of Traveller communities from a critical lifeworld-in-system perspective.

Conclusion

The sense of how one participates, converses and acknowledges the other is central to the growth of both personal and Traveller identities. This is, of course, not solely unique to Travellers—but applies to any group with a distinct language or 'form of life' (Wittgenstein) and a historically created communal identity.   Processes of learning, knowledge sharing, tradition maintaining and identity constructing or re-constructing within Traveller communities, however, demand certain levels of communicative competence— and facility in speaking the 'hidden languages' was once, and to some extent still is, one such competence. Hence, the importance of not forgetting and in re-claiming such languages in maintaining Traveller tradition, Traveller history and past, present and future Traveller identities.

Acknowledgements

I must acknowledge useful comments on earlier versions of this chapter by both editors of this volume, John Heneghan of the University of Limerick Traveller Access Project, and particularly Ann McMahon, visiting teacher for Traveller education in West Limerick.

References

Habermas, J. (1984), *The theory of communicative action—Vol 1: Reason and the rationalization of society*, T. McCarthy (trans.), Polity, Cambridge.

——. (1987a), *The theory of communicative action—Vol 2: Lifeworld and System: A critique of functionalist reason*, T. McCarthy (trans.), Polity, Cambridge.

——. (1987b), *The philosophical discourse of modernity*, F. Lawrence, (trans.), Polity, Cambridge.

——. (1996), *Between facts and norms*, W. Rehg, (trans.), Polity, Cambridge.

Henriksen, L.B., Nørreklit, L., Jørgensen, K.M., Christensen, J.B. and O'Donnell, D. (2004), *Dimensions of change - Conceptualising reality in organisational research*, Copenhagen Business School Press, Copenhagen.

Honneth, A., Knödler-Bunte, E. and Widmann, A. (1981), "The dialectics of rationalization: An interview with Jürgen Habermas", *Telos*, Vol. 49: 5-31.

McDonagh, Winnie (2000), "A Traveller woman's perspective on education", In F. Murphy, C. McDonagh & E. Sheehan (Ed.), *Travellers: Citizens of Ireland*, The Parish of the Travelling People, Dublin: 148-155.

O'Donnell, D. (1999), "Habermas, critical theory, and *selves*-directed learning", *Journal of European Industrial Training*, Vol. 23 Nos. 4/5: 251-261.

——. (2004), "Theory and method on intellectual capital creation: Addressing communicative action through relative methodics", *Journal of Intellectual Capital*, Vol. 5 No. 2: 294-311.

O'Donnell, D. and Henriksen, L.B. (2002), "Philosophical foundations for a critical evaluation of the social impact of ICT", *Journal of Information Technology*, Vol. 17 No. 2: 89-99.

O'Donnell D. and Porter, G. (2003), "Making space for communities of practice: Creating intellectual capital through communicative action", In M. Beyerlein, C. McGee, G.D. Klein, J.E. Nemiro, and L. Broedling, (Ed.), *The Collaborative Work Systems Fieldbook*, Jossey-Bass/Pfeiffer, San Francisco, CA.: 375-387.

Trainees of St. Joseph's Training Centre (2000), "Young Travellers experience of school", In F. Murphy, C. McDonagh & E. Sheehan (Ed.), *Travellers: Citizens of Ireland*, The Parish of the Travelling People, Dublin: 156-163.

Wittgenstein, L. (2001/1953), *Philosophical investigations* (3rd Edn.), Blackwell, Oxford.

CHAPTER EIGHT

PAVEES AND MUSCERS:[1]
POLICE DIVERSITY TRAINING,
IRISH TRAVELLERS, AND THE LIMITS
OF BRITISH PLURALISM

COLM POWER

Introduction

This essay examines the treatment of Irish Travellers by a number of police forces in Britain and focuses in particular on the manner in which Irish Travellers challenge the black/white binary in relation to ethnicity training, operational methods training and training for police diversity in the wake of the Macpherson Report (1999). It provides a brief background to some facets of Irish Traveller ethnicity and outlines the extent to which Britain's Irish Traveller population have been socially marginalised and ethnically disqualificied against and the consequences of same. This sets the context for a discussion of policing and concerns as relating to service delivery as relating groups with a culture of nomadism.

The essays also focuses on Irish Travellers' experiences as documented in the author's recent qualitative in-depth empirical research (Power, 2004). The author uses interviews with the police (at a number of levels), other service providers and Irish Travellers to explore both overt and long-established ignorance and prejudice in police practices vis-à-vis Irish Travellers and the adverse impact this has on Travellers' life chances. The essay also outlines in

---

[1] Some Irish Travellers call themselves Pavees and refer to the police as "Muscers" in their own language, known as Cant or Gammon.

brief 'who' the Irish Travellers are, and highlights some aspects of racism and discrimination as faced by this community in contemporary Britain. A particular focus is on institutional racism as relating to operational policing in the wake of the recommendations of the Macpherson Report (1999). It then examines some specific issues which relate to both overt and individual and institutionally discriminatory practices in two English police forces as experienced by Irish Travellers.

This essay is based on primary qualitative research conducted as part of the 'Room to Roam: Britain's Irish Travellers' project (2004), a Community-Fund resourced research project.[2] This three-year project involved focus groups and 140 in-depth interviews with Irish Travellers and related service providers (health, education, social services, local politicians, voluntary services, police and criminal justice system services) in both a Southern English Metropolis (SEM) and a Major English Northern City (MENC). All respondents, institutional actors and locations as cited in the Report and in this essay have were altered in order to protect the identities of the research respondents. This research aimed to assess the impact of social marginalisation, ethnic disqualification, and criminalisation on Travellers' health and life-chances and to suggest positive policy and practice alterations where appropriate. The criminal justice element of the research project was enhanced after the project began as a response to growing anecdotal and focus-group evidence suggesting that the relatively high numbers of Irish Travellers in the Criminal Justice System were being discriminated against as Travellers, but were also being ethnically disqualified against by institutions such as the police. The primary qualitative data used in this paper draws on in-depth interviews with Irish Travellers and police operatives at a number of service levels including diversity trainers, community police, middle ranking operational officers and civilian police advisors on ethnicity in both MENC and SEM. These interviews are analysed so as to investigate the extent of institutional racism and operational prejudices within the system, a racism which runs from the policy stage, through to training and into the arena of operational practice. This sets the context for an examination of the contradictions in the state's legal and policy formulations, contradictions that underpin anti-Irish Traveller racism in British society. By examining the manner in which by a powerful institution such as the police - (who operate at the raw interface between and state and society) - reproduce and amplify negative stereotypes of Irish and other Travellers it is possible to see how race relations can be consistently undermined despite the existence of race

---

[2] This project was run by a consortium that included Action Group for Irish Youth, BIAS Irish Travellers Project, and University of Surrey - St. Mary's College.

relations and equality legislation that is intended to protect such legally recognised minority ethnic groups.

The SEM police operational area examined here covers a large metropolis that is divided into thirty-two boroughs/police areas overseen by a large centralised bureaucratic structure situated in central SEM. SEM and MENC have large but generally 'invisible' Irish Traveller populations. MENC's periphery has a number of authorised sites but the city itself has only one small Local Authority site. Until recently many unauthorized encampments existed in this area also Urban regeneration and the consequent commodification of land has closed off many of the traditional stopping places for Travellers. Partly as a consequence of this, the vast majority of Irish Travellers live in settled-type accommodation such as houses, flats and hostels – though many move regularly through the housing system and some migrate occasionally to other British cities or to Ireland. There are many others also who continually to be seasonally nomadic (see Power, 2004: Section 2.3).

Who are Pavees/Irish Travellers?

Irish Travellers' distinctive way of life, values, culture and traditions manifest themselves in Traveller 'nomadism', the importance of the extended family, their own language, – Cant or Gammon - and the unique nature of their economies. Irish Travellers have also played a significant role in maintaining unique aspects of Irish culture.   Historically, Irish Travellers have been self-employed in businesses such as horse trading, seasonal farm-work, rural crafts, selling domestic goods door-to-door, and as herbalists, musicians and tinsmiths. Traditional employment opportunities - have in recent decades, in particular - been radically altered by agricultural change, mass production, and mass consumerism.   Travellers' employment patterns have shifted to casual and entrepreneurial forms of building work, tarmacking, furniture and antique dealing, and scrap metal collection among others (Power, 2004). Street begging and petty crime amongst Travellers is a minor problem but Travellers as a whole have been routinely labelled as petty criminals by many settled people and sections of the media (Rutter, 1997; Acton, 1994). Migration to major cities in Britain has increased in the last half century as many Irish Travellers' traditional economies have collapsed with the modernisation of settled society.   Their nomadic rights have been severely curtailed by criminal justice legislation and settled people's resistance to their way of life both in Ireland and Britain. Conflict has arisen between urban settled denizens, various municipal authorities, police forces, and all Traveller ethnic groups over modes of living and access to scarce resources (Power, 2004; Sibley, 1995).   Prejudice and racism from both institutional and societal sources including large elements of the settled Irish community in Britain, has rendered Travellers almost powerless politically.

Accurate statistics on Irish Travellers are difficult to obtain as those pursuing a nomadic lifestyle are largely absent from Census returns and those living in settled forms of accommodation are not defined as a separate ethnic group. Ethnic monitoring of Irish Travellers does not occur in the CJS in any systematic form. Estimates for the Irish Traveller population in Britain are scarce. No government information is collected on specific Traveller population numbers, age, gender, or ethnicity – therefore no accurate government statistics exist for Irish Travellers or other Traveller and Gypsy groups in Britain (Hickman and Walter, 1997: 20-21). Since the Criminal Justice and Public Order Act (CJPOA 1994) the statutory duty on local authorities to provide sites has been removed,, very few new sites are being built to compensate for site closures and Traveller population growth. Population estimates for Travellers and Gypsies in the United Kingdom range anywhere between 90,000 and 120,000 (Niner, 2002: 10). The age profile of Irish Travellers is exceptionally young: they tend to marry early and families average eight children, so the population is growing quickly (Ibid: 9-10). Irish Travellers form a large proportion of the nomadic and semi-nomadic Traveller population in Britain. The above estimate does not include the large numbers (probably the majority) of Irish Travellers who have been forced from their traditional nomadic way of life due to a lack of trailer sites and the virtual outlawing of nomadism in England and Wales and are living either temporarily or permanently in variious settled forms of accommodation (Power, 2004). The large disparities in population estimates can be partly explained by high internal mobility rates, but also by the (largely under researched) phenomenon of Irish Traveller migration between Britain and Ireland (north and south) and also into continental Europe.

The legal context of policing Irish Travellers in Britain

The Public Order Act (1986) and the more draconian CJPOA (1994) have virtually outlawed the traditional nomadic/semi-nomadic lifestyles of all Traveller groups in England and Wales. Unauthorised stopping on traditionally used marginal land and roadside verges was criminalised, and the duty on local authorities to provide permanent trailer sites was also removed as was the central government provision of statutory grants for local authorities to build permanent sites. Part Five of the CJPOA also extended the powers contained in the Public Order Act 1986 (Section 39), giving the police draconian powers against trespassers. The CJPOA (1994) virtually outlaws nomadic and semi-nomadic lifestyles. Its anti-trespass provisions are often invoked against Irish Travellers on unofficial or illegal encampments bringing them into confrontation with police forces in Britain. Evictions of Travellers amounted to 236 in 1995 and 187 in 1996, thirty-three percent of which were carried out under the CJPOA (1994) (Clements and Smith, 1997). The Association of Chief Police Officers' (ACPO) (cited in Ibid, 1997: 18) official reaction to the elements of the CJA 1994 Act that criminalised Travellers' nomadic activities was to express their:

> ...resistance to the proposal to 'criminalise' the act of living in a caravan. It is felt to be a unique situation to proscribe a way of life, formerly accepted as being within the law and then to introduce penalties. Whilst recognizing the problems, the police do not have any great difficulty in 'policing' the Gypsy and itinerant communities.

Many Travellers' reaction to local authority and police harassment of small nomadic groups (usually between two and six trailers) is to travel and congregate in much larger groups of fifty or more trailers. This tactic serves to prevent harassment or intimidation by settled vigilantes or police which can result in the confiscation of Travellers' trailers, generators and other vital equipment, often during the night (Irish Travellers cited in Power, 2004). However, the appearance of large trailer groups also encourages sections of the media and the political élite to exacerbate sedentary moral panics about 'Traveller invasions' and supposedly locally related 'crime waves', panics which are more aptly construed historically by Sharpe (1983: 210) as state-sponsored 'enforcement waves'.

Sergeant Plummer (cited in Power, 2004: 76), a MENC Police diversity trainer, concurs with ACPO's opinions stated above and acknowledges as predictable Travellers' reaction to the law's implementation:

> [W]hen the 1994 Act [CJPOA] came in regarding moving people off ground, one of the things that occurred to me then was a lot of chief constables of police didn't always use those powers because there was a massive concern about some of the backlash that would actually [come] from the community.

Also notable is the reticence of some police forces about certain provisions of the CJPOA (1994). For instance, a MENC-based bailiff (cited in Ibid: 77) who specialised in Traveller evictions complained about the lack of support he received during evictions from police forces across the north of England. There is a marked reluctance to use this legislation by senior officers in some police forces due to its extremely draconian provisions and its sectarian focus on the very fabric of culturally nomadic groups.

The criminalisation of nomadic and semi-nomadic Travellers' cultural and economic way of life and the demonisation of Irish Travellers throughout sedentary society mean that highly discretionary legislation such as the Police and Criminal Evidence Act (PACE 1984) may be used disproportionately and in a discriminatory way against Irish Travellers. Sergeant McCarthy (cited in Ibid: 80) of the SEM police college explains that often when police stop Travellers:

> ...they don't know what they are looking for so the police officer [thinks]: "I want to quickly establish myself in ... control ... if I can latch onto a criminal offence that's a starter". From that point on he thinks: "...I can deal with that where I've got more ... control." And because of ... PACE Section 25 ... if you weren't satisfied with the person's name and address ... that gives you power to arrest them and then 'slow-time' deal with what you don't know enough about back at the station. It might be about possession of equipment [or]... an Irish registration, so you don't know enough about the legitimacy of national driving documents. But once you are back in the station in "slow-time" you can actually deal with this more thoroughly. The experiences that most police officers have are short negative [ones] ... society almost condones you to do whatever with a transient group: "Whatever you do that gets rid of them, its ok by us".

Sergeant Plummer (cited in Ibid), a MENC Police veteran, discusses how his own received prejudices about Irish Travellers developed and concurs with the opinion of Sergeant McCarthy - as regards the manner in which) - these extra police powers now encourage police to intervene and look for criminality where previously they used their discretion not to do so where it was deemed inappropriate:

> [Operationally as a police officer] I only had about three or four experiences [with Travellers]. I worked in outer MENC, but when I go back to [19]83 ... you had an awful lot of Travelling families who moved into one particular estate and ... it ghettoised it so much that when they did it up they changed the names of the streets to ... cover-up. One of the prejudices that was handed down to officers was [when] you'd see what was perceived to be a Travellers vehicle: "Don't bother stopping them, they won't have any documents and you won't ever be able to serve a summons on them". Now when Section 25 PACE came out ... this changed things because ... you can arrest anybody for anything under certain conditions ... [if] the name and address was unsuitable [for] ... serving summonses... You impound the vehicle, arrest them - bring them in to establish where they are. On one occasion the prosecutions department issued summonses there and then when [Travellers had] been brought in... They presume [Travellers] will disappear and not come back. ... So Section 25 gives a huge amount of discretion ... for dealing with Travellers.

A complex matrix of legislation affects how Travellers are policed. A legal system which developed historically focussed on the centrality of exclusive land ownership, the marginalisation of common ownership and common land, the promotion of sedentary accommodation and lifestyles, and a consequent criminalisation of traditional nomadic rights. This process has left Travellers and Gypsies at loggerheads with the police both in terms of the criminal and civil legal systems, but also as a consequence of deeply-ingrained prejudices that frequently inform the deployment of police discretionary powers.

Post-Macpherson policing policies and Irish Travellers

Such social concepts - including an understanding of the historical conditions which contributed to the development of white ethnic minorities including Travellers and Gypsies - are almost completely absent from debates about ethnicity and race in Britain (Parekh, 2000). A Metropolitan Police Authority (MPA) member (Irish Community Consultation meeting, 4 May 2001) admitted that the MPA had not considered or discussed the Irish Community as a whole (one of the largest ethnic minority groups in England) in the context of the Macpherson Report (1999) and institutionalised racism – not to mention Irish Travellers or other culturally nomadic groups. The Parekh Report (2000: 129) found that:

> Black and Irish people are differentially treated at all stages of the criminal justice system, from policing on the streets through to sentencing and imprisonment.

Hillyard (1993; see also Hickman and Walter, 1997) recognised that the Irish in Britain have been understood historically as a security threat by the British state and its security apparatus. This, coupled with the black/white binary that equates ethnicity with non-white groups only, has created institutional blocks to treating the Irish and Irish Travellers as a minority ethnic group as opposed to a high-risk security concern. Irish Travellers are exceptional in that they suffer from double suspicion and double discrimination both as part of the Irish Diaspora and as Travellers with a nomadic disposition (Parekh, 2000: 34).

Evidence from one of SEM Police's diversity trainers indicates that British police culture is ill-prepared to engage with the idea of Irish ethnicity not to mention that the specific ethnicity of Irish Travellers. Sergeant McCarthy (cited in Power, 2004: 80) has an Irish background and teaches at the SEM Police Training College. He (cited in Ibid; see also Hillyard, 1993; Hickman and Walter, 1997) makes a connection between the negative stereotypes of Irish

Travellers and those stereotypes that have been applied historically to the settled Irish community in Britain:

> I was intrigued by the link between Irishness and Irish Traveller and some of the stereotypes that attach to Irishness. ... [An unmistakably Irish name] was enough for people to get on your case in the past... [SEM Police has] about thirty-thousand [officers], but of those police officers just 0.5 percent identify as white-Irish. Either we are not recruiting [Irish] or people from that background don't identify, which is alarming given that in the SEM area there is probably a million people [with] an Irish background... [T]here's no Irish police staff association where now we have ... Italian, Greek, Jewish, black police associations running for a long time.[3] I [considered] starting an Irish police association ... [but would it be] all things Irish culturally or ... subversive to further political things and ... you think well this is ... a can of worms [so do] I really want to get involved...

The link between Irish identity, state security, a suspect community and Irish Travellers is a recurring theme with many Irish Traveller respondents in the 'Room to Roam' research and also in this chapter.

Overtly and at a central bureaucratic and policy level SEM police have instituted a wide range of reviews and policy initiatives since the Macpherson Report (1999) was published. Macpherson (Ibid: 20) defined institutional racism as the:

> Collective failure of an organisation to provide an appropriate and professional service to people because of their colour, culture or ethnic origin. It can be seen or detected in processes, attitudes and behaviour which amount to discrimination through unwitting, prejudice, ignorance, thoughtlessness and racist stereotyping, which disadvantage minority ethnic staff.

As part of these post-Macpherson initiatives SEM Police set up a Police Diversity Directorate (PDD) to develop and advise on policies in relation to the issues of ethnicity and race. However, areas of particular interest to Travellers such as public order policy remain the sole responsibility of an unrelated department. Sergeant Humphry (cited in Power, 2004: 77) works for SEM PDD and has special responsibility for Traveller related questions:

> I work for the Policy and the Planning Unit [PPU] which is a bit of a misnomer ... I'm responsible for pushing forward the SEM Police diversity policy on Gypsies and Travellers. ... The Directorate covers the whole of SEM, but [its] got no prescriptive powers at all - it advises Boroughs. Boroughs ... produce their own policies and they've got their own systems liaisons officer ... the

---

[3] There have been recent, definite moves within SEM police to establish a staff association based on Irish ethnicity.

Directorate merely advises on ways of doing things. That really is one of the problems with the Diversity Directorate ... it has no prescriptive powers. ... I help to do what I call Community Intelligence briefings... [an] example would be ... a large Traveller funeral - I ... speak ... with the families, advise the police officers of local customs and what they can expect because many police officers have never policed a Traveller/Gypsy funeral. The idea of people wailing at the side of the grave, they wouldn't know how to deal with it...

Here Humphry sees no incongruity between the needs of a Traveller family to grieve for a lost loved one with dignity and the presumed public order threat a funeral poses for the police. Are public order police tactics appropriate for family funerals even if large by settled standards? Can't the police find a more sensitive means to police Traveller funerals?

An Irish Traveller's (cited in Ibid) description of policing operations at his family's traditional cemetery resembles those used at paramilitary funerals in Northern Ireland:

If there is a funeral there's a lot of police. Most of my people are buried over here in [Oakshire]. Every time I've been to that graveyard there are thousands of police - all the roads blocked off.

Humphry's description of the PPD's impotency and the PPU's role within that nexus of policy development and implementation structures has disturbing resonances with many the historical attempts to legislate positively for Travellers where the 'buck was passed' from central to local government as with the Caravan Sites Act (1968), or where recommendations were non-mandatory as with the Caravan Sites and Control of Development Act (1960). SEM Police PPD, despite all the post Macpherson hype, is an advisory organ separate from the real policy makers like 'D12' Public Order Department, while the real power to act and change operationally resides with the local Borough Commander. The Macpherson Report's (1999: section 6.13; also Whyte, June 2002) explanation of institutional racism laid particular emphasis on its unwitting, unconscious and unintentional nature. The report (Ibid: Section 6.17) located institutional racism in the Metropolitan police as being rooted in ignorance of *'the behaviour and cultural traditions of people or families from minority ethnic communities ... [and] stereotyping of black people as potential criminals or troublemakers'*. Whyte (June 2002: 7; also McLaughlin, 2000) asserts that institutional racism in a policing context:

...involved the simultaneous targeting of black communities by the police and other branches of the state alongside a project of political and cultural assimilation ... at the centre of the strategies of assimilation ... were community-police relations forums that started to evolve in the 1960s.

It seems that virtually the same formula that Whyte outlines above for black people is being extended to non-black ethnic minority groups like Irish Travellers – a 'difficult to reach group' who have not as yet developed the political and organisational networks extant in many black and south Asian communities. But how have the new post Macpherson *'community-police relations forums'* developed, and have they impacted positively on relations between Black and minority ethnic communities and the police?

Operational policing and Irish Travellers

Irish Travellers, in particular, have been routinely labelled as petty criminals and socially undesirable by many powerful definers in society. Yet Morris and Clements (1999: 33) state that:

> ACPO (Association of Chief Police Officers) continues to assert that they have no disproportionate problems with criminality in the Travelling populations, and the continuing presumptions stem largely from stereotyping.

Conflict has arisen between urban settled denizens, local authorities, police forces, and Irish Travellers as urbanisation dissolved the traditional socio-economic ties that bound nomadic and settled communities together (McCarthy, 1994; Sibley, 1995). As a result their traditional nomadic rights (and those of similar groups) in Britain have been severely curtailed by the increased commodification of marginal land, growing prejudice from sedentary society, and the CJPOA (1994) among other factors.

Traveller Liaison Officers (TLOs) are not envisaged as an integral constituent of SEM police's response to Traveller concerns in the wake of the Macpherson report, but are really part of a public order initiative related to the policing of illegal Traveller encampments. As with many Traveller-related initiatives the "buck" seems to have been transferred from the police central authority to a form of local area management. The PDD can advise local Borough Commanders about the cultural sensitivities of Travellers, but the nature of TLO's liaison remit is decided by SEM Police Public Order Branch, while the interpretation, commitment and operational trajectory is left to local Borough Commanders. So there is little continuity or networking built into the TLO's role. The designated TLOs in both northwest SEM research areas took some time to locate and felt unable to contribute to this research due to their deficient seniority. The research team had great difficulty finding out the identity of the TLOs and received no response from local management to requests for assistace with this research (research diary cited in Power, 2004: 81). Sergeant Humphry (cited in Ibid) of SEM PDD comments on the concept, recruitment and actual function of TLOs:

> SEM Police is a big organisation. I lead on a diversity aspect ... D12 lead on the public order part of Gypsies and Travellers. [D12] were responsible for publishing the policy on unauthorised camping ... that policy created the post of TLOs, but the role of the TLO ... was to liaise with Local Authorities about Travellers, the role wasn't designed for liaison with Travellers. ... [T]he policy was about unauthorised encampment rather than specifically about Gypsies and Travellers. TLOs [are mainly] a part-time post within other responsibilities - Borough Commanders ... had a choice. West SEM is a good example, [it] has a full-time TLO - PC Noonan. Now he's something of an exception as he's appointed under that Public Order policy notice ... but he's developed that into a community-based role with the support of his Borough Commander ... Travellers and their groups feel the role of TLOs need to be redefined ... if you call it a TLO then they should liaise with Travellers.

PC Noonan (cited in Ibid) is a full-time TLO in west SEM.[4] Noonan, a beat officer with an Irish background, was asked to expand his duties to cover Traveller sites in his area eighteen months ago. He believes most officers do not want the TLO post and he himself occasionally feels stressed and isolated. He thinks that depression, fear and substance abuse is common amongst Travellers and the abuse of illicit drugs now predominates over alcohol. He also believes that the culture of Travellers gives them a propensity to crime and that travelling is a ploy to commit crime that goes undetected. Noonan alleged that large groups of Travellers encamp and take stolen cars etc. back to illegal sites for dismantling and sale. Noonan said that 4,000 caravans were stolen in the UK last year and he estimates ninety percent of those thefts were committed by Travellers. Noonan believes that many Travellers are extremely wealthy from various ventures including crime. The walls of Noonan's office at the police station are covered in photos of Travellers wanted for serious crimes. He asserts that the more common Traveller-related crimes include stealing household goods and selling them at boot-sales, selling stolen video cameras at the roadside and then swapping the bag so buyers get a bag full of soap instead of the camera. Noonan believes that few Travellers earn a legitimate living and are generally given to idleness. TLO Noonan estimates that some young Traveller males make up to £1,800 per week from benefits fraud and other dealings and that many Irish Travellers claim Child Benefit in Ireland and collect it at ATMs in Britain as the payments are higher in the Irish Republic and there are no links between the two benefit systems. O'Flynn (1993: 46-55) presents much evidence that contradicts Noonan's assertions, and documents the difficulties

---

[4] He declined a recorded interview, and therefore notes were taken by the researcher.

and barriers to Social Security payments experienced by many Irish Travellers. It is somewhat surprising that someone with Noonan's trenchant anti-Irish Traveller views has been chosen to be a SEM police TLO.

Sergeant McCarthy (cited in Power, 2004: 82) believes that the anti-Traveller prejudices prevalent in society generally are amplified within the police by the very nature of policing:

> In all of society there's unhealthy attitudes towards Travelling people that are based on very little information and even police officers don't have that much contact and ... the unfortunate thing is the few contacts they have, tend to be negative ones and that colours the judgement for all.

A twenty-five-year-old Irish Traveller in Baton Prison (cited in Ibid) describes his experience of 'street justice' with police in SEM:

> The police ... think automatically that they can stick a burglary on us. ... I've had loads of beatings off police ... I broke about twenty cars [joyriding] but they couldn't charge me, [they] handcuffed me for Godsake and set the dogs on me in the back of the police station. ... It's terrible for Travellers in [certain SEM boroughs] ... they can spot Travellers.

The police are part of society and consequently are part of and party to societal power politics. Reiner (1992: 137) argues that policing practice is:

> ...differentiated according to the power of particular groups to cause problems for the police... [thus the]... power structure of a community, and the views of its elites, are important sources of variation in policing styles.

The crucial aspect of the relationship between the police and most of the majority sedentary community is the police perception that significant power elites exist within the community apart from those marginalised through a combination of geographical, ethnic and class dispositions. Conversely PACE (1984) stop-and-search and other intrusive powers like the CJPOA (1994) are part of a generalised surveillance of 'high risk' socially excluded groups like Irish Travellers.

Community engagement by the police?

An Irish Traveller woman (cited in Power, 2004: 78) thinks that Travellers should engage more with the authorities when they have complaints about the police: '*I think that Travellers don't complain enough about these incidents. The police attitude is "dirty gippos'*. Sergeant Humphry (cited in Ibid) of SEM PDD describes how Traveller's policing concerns are being incorporated into the community consultation networks that have developed since Macpherson was published in 1999:

> Each Borough has got its own Independent Advisory Group (IAG). They are groups of people who live in the community, represent the community ... they advise the Borough Commanders of what's going on... There are also people called mediators who we are also looking to recruit from each Traveller community ... where you get incidents within the Travelling community. ... What you get with a mediator is again a trusted third party who stands between both groups [police and Travellers] and can represent ... the reasons why police are doing what they've got to do to Travellers and then Travellers can soon reflect these back to police - so hopefully you end up with is a middle path that doesn't annoy everybody... What they are advising is police officers who know nothing about the subject ... also advising Travellers who [know] nothing at all about police procedures. ... I don't think ... they are a grass [police informer]. ... In an ideal world it would be another Traveller [sic]. ... I think ... we will start getting people once trust is established.

Sergeant Plummer (cited in Ibid). a former diversity trainer at MENC Police College and now a sub-divisional trainer. has a more cynical slant on why MENC Police management are reluctant to acknowledge ethnicity and he links this to the selection 'process' for police 'community consultation representatives':

> Now my argument is - who are these community leaders? [Someone] from maybe the Asian communities come to the police station to make a complaint one day and ... the chief super[intendent] says: "Oh, come along to this meeting." And this guy then becomes the community leader, but who does he represent? Does he really represent the young people? And [police management] also used to link it in perhaps with the Imams in some of the mosques. ... What effect can this guy have ... would you go along to see the local priest or vicar to say we've got a problem with youths? ... It all links into ... values, and saying: "Well this is the way that [ethnic minorities] see the world", [and the police] not understanding that. And that is perpetuated on so many occasions by thinking "we've got a problem with the Travelling community – [so] we'll go and get the guy in from [them]..."

Here Plummer argues that there are no particular criteria for selection onto IAGs and he suspects the representative 'quality' of some of the members. He also intimates that 'representative' IAG members can be used by the police not only to deflect damaging criticism by the claim that the police consult with ethnic minority leaders, but also that IAGs have been used over time to negate Macpherson's (1999) label of institutional racism. Thereby, ethnic minorities again become 'the problem' while the police and CJS resume their function as the state's primary means of controlling groups excluded from the 'inclusive society' (McLaughlin, 2000; Whyte, 2002). Mr. Hijaz (cited in Power, 2004: 78-79), a civilian MENC Police Community Race Relations Officer, believes that the MENC IAG is not diverse enough, it has too many men and Asian members. Hijaz believes local politicians are *'a waste of time – always sticking up for the police'* (cited in Ibid: 79). One SEM IAG member confided to a researcher that they felt they were picked by the police because they were perceived as easy to manipulate – most of the members contributed little and nodded their assent to decisions taken by a small active core who dominated many initiatives (research diary cited in Ibid).

Inspector Wood (cited in Ibid) is a Community Affairs police officer in South MENC and he states that his job is that of building links with communities. However, he too, peddles the often-repeated official opinion that Travellers are the 'problem' as they are so 'difficult to reach':

> It's about. I know the sort of group [Irish Travellers] you are talking about ... in as much as they are difficult to make contact with... But it's extremely difficult ... if there is distrust from one side, then it means that whatever we do - not only the police but agencies such as the Council - if they don't want to access those services then ... there is little we can do... They can be quite transient, and they are quite invisible.   So ... we might not know that there is a particular preponderance of Travellers in an area ... they are just seen as problem families. ... I don't think the police ... differentiate between Irish people, Travellers, Gypsies whatever, but certainly certain sections of the community do cause problems. ... But ... we don't label people. ... We just treat each incident as it comes, but obviously each incident builds up a picture doesn't it?

MENC Police don't stereotype or label; their mode of operation involves building up a picture of a community over time, one which surely develops into a negative representation of the group if no positive engagement with that community is sought by the police. By locating police within the multi-agency context Wood tries to bolster the legitimacy of the police perspective on Travellers.

Scotland Yard first established a London-wide IAG (with local borough equivalents) to consult with ethnic communities in the Metropolitan Police Service (MPS) area in response to the Macpherson Report (1999). However, four prominent members of the IAG (Dr. Ben Bowling law lecturer, Andrea Cork MPS race relations trainer, Jennifer Douglas Home Office advisor, and Kirpal Sahota, a forensic psychiatrist) all resigned together in early 2001 and simultaneously issued a joint statement which accused the MPS of subverting its original community-engagement remit:

The IAG has ceased to function independently, or collectively. We cannot in good faith continue to be part of a group that is supposed to be comprised of the organisation's "sternest critics", when this is clearly no longer the case. ... We feel that the IAG process is no longer contributing to the restoration of confidence and trust in the MPS in any meaningful way. We feel that we can no longer remain members of the IAG because it is now explicitly controlled by the police. As a result it can no longer claim to offer independent advice and is, therefore, failing in its responsibility to improve policing for Londoners (cited in Dodd, Guardian, 13 February 2001).

Interestingly, Whyte (2002: 40) asserts that the most serious problem from a state/police perspective is not police racism or institutional racism, but '*the reluctance of the black communities to co-operate with the police*'. McLaughlin (2000) argues that police discourse since the 1960s has regularly re-emphasised this 'difficult to reach' aspect of particular ethnic minority communities in response to social unrest.

Sergeant Humphry (cited in Power, 2004: 79) of SEM PDD envisages developing and extending a system of 'third party reporting' to enhance the police service to Traveller and Gypsy communities. This development would tackle unreported crime and endeavour to develop trust between Traveller and Gypsy communities over time:

I will ... push ... third party reporting. ... It allows groups of people [or] individuals who either have no particular faith in the police or the police have been unable to deal with their problems ... [to report] any crime at all to a neutral trusting third party [who] then passes that information on to police for investigation. ... [Q]uite a lot of minority groups are victims of what isn't being reported - experience has shown with the black and Asian community that that's the case. ... We are pushing this ... system specifically [for] Gypsies and Travellers. Travellers are really the last group that society ... thinks its fair game to have a pop at. ... Once we've started winning people's confidence we can go further with more imaginative schemes...

An Irish Traveller male (cited in Ibid) gives his opinion on what it means for someone from his community to report a crime to the police:

[F]or example someone cuts me up ... if I go to the police then I mark myself and the family is marked. ... It wouldn't be just me and him having problems, it would be his brothers as well. And then it would be my brothers and then outsiders come in and start getting involved... No you can't go to the police - you can't! If ... you go to the police you're known as a grass, a squealer, and then that will go against you for the rest of your life among Travellers.

Sergeant Humphry (cited in Ibid: 80) is creating a space for Traveller issues in police diversity training while also trying to develop a more positive image of Travellers within the SEM Police force, but he has difficulties recruiting members with a Traveller background as mentors for new recruits:

> We've got a Diversity Training School ... if you've got a ... big Traveller population in the Borough ... senior management will say: "In our second phase we would like a big input on Gypsies and Travellers..." I placed an advert in the internal [police] newspaper [for officers with a Traveller/Gypsy background]. It's been two months and only eight people feel confident enough to come forward ... so it's fairly limited. I am hoping to use these police officers who've identified as having a Travelling background like a support network for those Travellers who do join...

The Morris Inquiry (2004) commissioned by the Metropolitan Police Service was set up to examine professional standards and employment issues in the light of concerns relating to unfairness, disproportionality and discrimination in the way that some employment matters were dealt with as regards Black and Asian officers – no mention was made of 'non-visible' minority ethnic groups such as Travellers and Gypsies however.

Community policing and Irish Travellers

Her Majesty's Inspector of Constabulary (1999:9) with particular responsibility for police, race and community relations suggested that: *'what commentators and journalists have referred to as "the canteen culture" . . . . . is as misleading as it is mischievous'*. Yet there is no doubt that police occupational culture at all levels is grounded in received or 'commonsense' assumptions and prejudices at the operational level, and these are a crucial determinant of how all policy initiatives are translated into practice and are clearly the foremost barrier to change (McConville et al 1991; Chatterton 1993). Sergeant Plummer (Power, 2004: 83) explains that prejudices concerning Irish Travellers and Gypsies are deeply rooted in MENC Police culture:

> When we start looking at peoples prejudices people are not going to open-up in certain areas, but one particular area where people felt quite ok about airing their prejudices would be the Travelling community. They will be quite happy to say: "Yea, I don't like Travellers – can't stand them. Because they are all thieves, and they will always have a story." It was flagged up at [College] by our trainers that there was an acceptance that it was ok to be prejudiced against Travellers.

In contrast PC Tudor (cited in Ibid: 84), a MENC Police Youth and Community Officer, comes across as concerned and interested in reaching out to 'hard to reach' nomadic ethnic groups, this in spite of the fact that negative stereotypes of Irish Travellers still permeate much of his discourse:

> I mean we could go back to your Travelling family again where maybe the males in the family do like to drink ... and they come home and they have an argument with the wife ... about anything ... and there's bricks going through the window.

Again, the following comment from PC Tudor (cited in Ibid) exonerates many Traveller parents from their children's criminal activity, but implicates others by insinuation/association:

> Half the time the adults of some of the children who go out stealing, having accidents, being chased by the police, arrested, detained and put on remand, maybe don't want them to do that... they are afraid...

MENC Police have not as yet developed a TLO network such as that which is used by SEM Police. Inspector Wood (cited in Ibid), MENC Community Affairs officer, explains that Travellers are not particularly prone to criminality, but that the police are driven by the reported prejudices of some often-vocal members in the settled community:

> If somebody had whatever stolen ... they may blame those [Traveller] folk down the road. Given that they suspect, we are duty bound to follow that up. ... [I]n the areas I have worked, I would say it's not the Travellers that have done the criminal acts. They quite often do other anti-social things but not necessarily criminal things. So people may think they lower the tone of an area, but I don't necessarily think that converts itself into criminality. If you are talking about driving without documents then ... it is the most common [offence] and mainly young men. [Our officers] might have had information that cars are being driven without insurance, without road tax ... it should all be intelligence led -but it's not just: "he looks like [a Traveller]."

Wood thus validates police intelligence-gathering protocol despite admitting earlier that this can be based on prejudice. Similarly, PC Tudor (cited in Ibid), a Police Youth and Community Officer for twelve years in North MENC, gives an example of how as a Community Officer he used to collect 'intelligence' about the presence of Irish Travellers in his beat area – again as directly linked to alleged crime as reported by non-Traveller residents:

> [T]he neighbours would hint at it, then the local bobbies would hint at it. ... They would say: "We've got huge car crime lately [in] this couple of streets." I know we are being judgmental, but sometimes people are right, aren't they? They [the police] go look and ... at forty-two will be your Travelling family.

PC Tudor explains how his job is now focusing more on young people already in the Youth Justice System, while this approach to community policing also involves a drive to improve police efficiency as Tudor (cited in Ibid) explains as follows:

> It's tending to go away from traditional community policing ... into crime solving and crime management unified in operational policing ... [so] crime "stats" ... lead me ... to look at reducing car crime. ... The best way is to get into your schools and ... community groups. ... dealing with the young people that have been involved with car crime when they've been through the arrest stage... We try and give them an alternative ... We do educational stuff based around teamwork just through football ... instead of being individuals ... we get them to work as a team. ... You look at an area, at the problem... say its burglary and then you go in there and you think: "How can I link with ... young people" ... Its about changing attitudes and about confronting other ones ... [We] look at things on a divisional basis foremostly to reduce the amount of calls to police... to [bring] officers stress levels down and so sickness levels come down.

Tudor (cited in Ibid: 84-85) admits that the recent changes to his community policing role and his targeting of 'at risk' youth in schools and youth clubs would probably overlook many young Irish Travellers who move regularly through housing and don't have particularly strong settled-community connections:

> [Travellers] have to lose their cultural background of being free and living off the land ... to [become] a neighbourhood based static kind of family and it doesn't work like that does it? ... If you've committed a serious offence you won't be bailed unless you've got a fixed address. ... My job lends itself to working with stable groups and there are so very few Travelling sites. They are all centred around housing now and ... if you did a survey of how long they [Travellers] stayed in one set of houses ... six to twelve months at a maximum.

Tudor asserts that Irish Travellers have to abandon their culture now and assimilate. MENC community policing in its old guise intervened with Travellers using intelligence garnered from local sedentary sources and likely to be influenced by negative perceptions and prejudices. The 'new' community approach misses many young Travellers through the limitations of its community outreach methods and only comes into contact with elements of the community who have already been implicated in criminality, thereby reinforcing perceptions of a criminogenic community.

The yawning gap between policy and practice evident in the MENC Police force at all operational level in the aftermath of Macpherson (1999) can be gauged from the response of which Mark (cited in Power, 2004: 85), a voluntary-sector outreach worker, received, when he gave a presentation about Irish Travellers on the MENC Police College diversity course. Sergeant Plummer (cited in Ibid) relates this episode:

> Mark was talking about how some young Traveller chap came over from ... Northern Ireland because he'd been threatened ... for stealing cars... He'd come over to MENC ... to live and the venom that came out: "But the man's a thief." We said: "Well yea, let's look at the situation. He's come over and we are trying to sort him out." [Police on race training say]: "But he shouldn't even be in this country ... why should he come here and get this [help]." All this stuff came out and Mark linked it into situations from southern Ireland ... and it was quite frightening to see... I've got representatives from the Muslim community [etc.] ... but when it came to Mark giving his input on Irish Travellers and the Irish community in general ... they felt quite open to express those feelings. I'm glad Mark said it to you because ... I sat back and I was shocked, I could not believe it. But on the other hand I could because I had experienced it before. That certainly did concern me in terms of the way that [police] view Irish Travellers - it certainly is negative... They put a difference between Gypsies and Tinkers and said: "Even the Irish don't like the Tinkers".

This training episode also underlines the black/white binary underpinning received 'commonsense' assumptions and prejudices at the police operational level. It also points to a particular prejudice directed at the Irish generally and one that is very prevalent in policing and the criminal justice system – i.e. the Irish as a suspect community – where security predominates over ethnicity in the social construction and perception of an immigrant community and its descendants (Hillyard, 1993; Hickman and Walter, 1997). This is particularly the case for Irish Travellers born in Britain as many retain strongly identifiable cultural attributes including their accent and various degrees of nomadism. The black/white binary has relegated the Irish from ethnic group to a politically 'suspect' community during thirty years of war in Northern Ireland and beyond; while Irish Travellers are systematically dealt with as a criminogenic group, pathologised as opposed to ethnicised as Sergeant Plummer (Power, 2004: 85-86) explains:

> I have never known a time ... that we are having a discussion on the community ... [anyone] say: "Oh lets invite a member of the Irish community... I just want to put this back to the whole issue of skin colour issues when we look at ... racial communities and ethnic communities ... obviously Travellers were included in that. They are not dark skinned so they are not seen that way. A quick example perhaps - I actually ended up going along to a tribunal some time ago and it was a crime prevention panel within the police service "Homewatch". And they were having burglaries in an area, so ... they sent out flyers saying:

"We've had a lot of burglaries in such and such an area. Observations please for Gypsy vehicles and Gypsy-looking people." So of course this went along to CRE who obviously dealt with it ... about ten, twelve years ago - I think it was a £10,000 pound fine for the police.

I tell this story [at Police College] and there are clients who say: "We are having similar problems and the [police] boss has told me to do that recently..." It was a situation where they'd had burglaries in area's and somebody said: "Oh it's the Gypsies, stick a flier out so that people know who to look for." They didn't do it of course, but these are people who have come to me and said the superintendent ... said: "We've had a lot of trouble with the Travellers, we are having burglaries in areas. It must be Travellers because of the sort of jobs that are going down. Let people know what's going on in the area." So I've said: "Well you know it's not right." He said: "I didn't think it was right in the first place." But again this links into the fact that people feel quite comfortable to do this... management tried to encourage it. Where there has been a spate of crime in an area ... [police management] sit round these meetings and say: "Right - who could be responsible for this." And someone will say: "Oh there are some Travellers have moved into so and so estate, I bet it's them. Right, let's fire something out." The people who came to me said: "Oh I stopped it from happening." Now whether they did stop it from happening ... I don't know ... but this came from their commander...

There has been some anecdotal evidence – prior to this - from Traveller support groups that police forces use a system of unofficial memorandums to 'warn' settled communities of the impending arrival of Travellers and the consequent possibility of a rise in crime in their particular area. This is the first evidence from the police (see Sergeant Plummer above) that this highly discriminatory and racist practice occurs. This practice subverts the RRAA (2001) and can hardly be construed as unwitting institutional police racism but as a deliberate and orchestrated racist targeting of an ethnic group instead. Plummer also indicates above that this deliberate racist targeting of Travellers is devised by some police managers who pressurise constables to carry out these illegal acts. A research contact in SEM also provided an example of one of these flyers that had been distributed to houses and left on vehicle windscreens in an area where Travellers had just set up an encampment (research diary cited in Ibid: 86)

Instead of blaming Macpherson's 'de-personalised institutional racism, or the 'bad apple in the barrel' thesis, or police 'canteen culture' racism, Plummer's evidence points to the commission of deliberate racist and discriminatory acts against a recognised ethnic group (Irish Travellers) by police managers. Sergeant Plummer (cited in Ibid: 86) continues:

[Police] will always come up with an example by saying it must be true because look: "I stopped a [Traveller] and they are always telling ... you lies..." So I will say: "I've had similar experiences, but ... with a whole bunch of other people as well." ... Nobody is going to admit to something if they ... can get away with something by giving you false details ... its just human behaviour it's not necessarily an ethnic [indicator]... I guarantee you I'll go into a classroom and start talking about Travellers and people will be coming out with examples ... the whole conception of ethnicity/race is all linked to seeing colour that's my ... experience in training.

Inspector Wood (cited in Ibid), a MENC Community Affairs officer, disagrees with Sergeant Plummer's analysis:

I have worked in east MENC and it did have a lot of Travellers and it's surprising the first time you stop [and] speak to them and they don't know their date of birth. You say: "How old are you?", and they say: "About thirty-two". ... Coming from my background it is hard to understand but ... that is no reason to brand them a criminal. No I wouldn't agree that officers brand Travellers or treat them any different ... just because somebody gives [an Irish Traveller] name, and says I live wherever, that's not a reason to refuse him bail.

Sergeant McCarthy (cited in Ibid: 87) of SEM Police outlines the need for anti-discriminatory legislation and sanctions as the only effective way to influence police (and sedentary) attitudes to Travellers positively:

There's still an unhealthy attitude towards the Travelling community ... because police officers or the police service reacts more effectively to law and also when the balance sheet indicates that we've got to do something. [If we're] being sued - we'll do something. So its law and the threat of litigation [and liability for] compensation makes us react. I think its trying to find more opportunities ... to interact on a positive front would pay dividends. But ultimately we are driven by performance on the case, by things like response times.

The recurring and unsubtle message for Travellers coming from sedentary society and its major institutions is that they ought to de-culturise themselves, settle in housing, and assimilate. If Irish Travellers live nomadically as is their way of life or aspiration, they are criminalised, but also – (ironically) - recognised as different and unique. When Travellers settle in accordance with sedentary "norms", they are shorn of their ethnicity by the state, its institutions and much of the settled population.

Police diversity training and Irish Travellers

One of the primary recommendations of the Macpherson report (1999) was that police forces should institute a meaningful diversity training programme for all of their staff. In the wake of inner city riots in the early 1980s the Scarman Report (1981) had called for police training aimed at *'an understanding of the cultural background of ethnic minority groups...'* and Lord Scarman, even then, felt satisfied enough to state in the report 'that improvements in police training are in hand' (Ibid: Sections 5.16, 5.17). However, Macpherson (1999: Section 6.45) has found eighteen years later that:

> ...not a single officer questioned before us in 1998 had received any training of significance in racism awareness and race relations throughout the course of his or her career.

Sergeant Plummer (cited in Power, 2004: 82) was a until recently a diversity trainer at MENC Police College and is now a sub-divisional trainer in MENC police:

> I've been in Greater MENC police for twenty-seven years. My first training roll was ... training recruits ... I have been on a six-week community and race relation trainers course ... on behalf of the Home Office after the Scarman Report [1981]. ... The ultimate aim [of training] is ... fair service delivery... If you are a police officer working in an urban area where ... most of the time you are dealing with criminals because the incidents are burglaries, assaults etc., it's very easy to believe that everybody in that area is a potential criminal... So the way that [police] come across [to locals] is: "[A]re the police ... really trying to help me out here or [have] they got some other hidden agenda in terms of their views on me." [P]rior to [19]81 [policing] was very much law based rather than interpersonal skills based... [After] Scarman police training ... started looking at the way that we deal with people and different cultures.

There was internal bureaucratic and institutional resistance to the changes proposed by the Scarman Report at that juncture in MENC Police according to Sergeant Plummer's (cited in Ibid) recollections:

> The senior management ... said: "Oh, do we really need this ... sort of stuff?" ... But in [19]94 it was [decided] to bring in community race relations training [with] specific aims and objectives ... primarily effective service delivery. I also assumed there was an issue regarding equality of opportunity. ... [T]he majority of people we trained were middle-management. ... [O]ne of the models ... from America was the paradigm of prejudice and discrimination: ... you can get a prejudice discriminator: somebody who has a prejudice and acts upon it. You can get a non prejudice discriminator - maybe a manager who ... didn't have a prejudice but discriminated because he or she thought ... "If I don't ... what will happen?" I used to say: "Well ... would there be a difference say between history taught in England as in Scotland ... William Wallace, was he a terrorist or was he a freedom fighter?" ... By the end of the day people come up and say: "I never thought about that before." ... In the seventies ... [police trainees] used

to go out [to] division for a couple of weeks and when they'd come back we'd
say: "Right... what do you see your key elements as?" [They'd say:] "Oh,
getting out there and get them locked up."

A Home Office report (1997) found many very basic problems with police
training, but the Macpherson Report (1999) revealed the generic problem of
translating written policy into action by operational ranks. These failures and a
lack of provision for police training all indicated the necessity for a complete
overhaul of police training regimes. Sergeant Plummer (cited in Power, 2004:
83), a former MENC diversity trainer, comments:

The most difficult thing that came out of Part Two of the Lawrence Inquiry was
the MENC Chief Constable saying: "Yes we do have institutionalised racism",
and that hurt. ... I have seen people get very angry in training sessions... The
media ... left out the bit where he said: "I accept that there's institutionalised
racism but the majority of my staff are doing a very good job under very hard
circumstances." People interpret institutionalised racism as saying you are all ...
racist rather than ... you've always provided services to [a] predominantly white
English community ... It was bad for morale because people literally hated the
Chief Constable and I found that I was defending what he said and I ended up
getting it in the neck and my colleagues did as well.

Inspector Wood (cited in Ibid), a Community Affairs officer in south MENC,
comments on how he feels the force has dealt with the rapid change post
Macpherson:

The police are one of the most receptive organisations going. ... There have been
a lot of changes, the police embraced them all. *[Interviewer's question] There
was resistance? [Wood's response]* No, no I don't think so. *[Interviewer's
question] Did the Chief Constable's admit the force was institutionally racist?
[Wood's response]* But to be honest, the term institutional racism, what does it
mean? And I am not sure that he realised ... the impact ... Now people have a
better understanding.

But Sergeant Plummer (Ibid) a former diversity trainer with MENC police
believes that the impact of Macpherson and its aftermath had an extremely
negative influence on training and other race-related initiatives such as racial
incident reporting:

I mean the hardest thing that people had to accept in "race group" was racist
incidents ... we were saying if somebody tells you it's a racist incident you've
got to report it as one regardless of whether you see it that way... [The police]
had no discretion ... for the first time ever we were saying: "It doesn't matter if
there isn't any evidence, put the form in". But the point that we wanted to get
across was investigate it, find out. But that didn't really come across... MENC

has got a large Jewish community racism can occur there, an Irish community as well where again people might have their prejudiced views... I think most [police] people saw it as a black and white issue... [T]here are two ways of doing this training. One way is by just going through the components without challenging any[thing] ... this is racism, this is sexism... so people will start getting the feedback sheet to say: "Wow this is good, no problems here." If ... you've gone deeper touching some sensitive areas, making people think - then they say: "Rubbish, I didn't buy that," because you've actually done what you are supposed to do. I made myself ill ... I was out for six months.

Sergeant Plummer sums up the real problem with police training regimes in Britain – i.e. resources and commitment. A six-week diversity training course is shrunk to two days and committed training teams are undermined by the impossibility of challenging embedded prejudice with so few resources and so little time.

Sergeant Plummer (cited in Ibid: 86) continues his description of police diversity training in the MENC force:

We used to have a quiz ... one of the questions was who are the largest ethnic [group] ... and they'd all say West Indians - they would never say the Irish community - so that really highlights it. ... If they [meet] ... working-class Irish they will be very tempted to think they are Tinkers... [Here Plummer himself uses the pejorative 'Tinkers' to describe Irish Travellers] You are speaking to somebody with an Irish accent, he comes up with [a Traveller] name, most bobbies are going to go "ding" and ... say: "Just hang on a minute mate." They do a check and if it came back "no trace" they would start thinking: "Hang on, is that your right date of birth." We are also told that the ... Tinker [sic] communities use more than one name ... these are the things that come out.

This is part of a trend toward 'actuarial' social control emphasising the management of high-risk groups rather than focusing on criminal offenders (see Feeley and Simon, 1994; Johnston, 2000). Sergeant Plummer (cited in Ibid: 86-87) comments again:

How do you measure how effective you've been in delivering that training? Do we look at that in the terms of racial incidents for reporting? Do we look at that the increase or decrease of complaints against the police on racial grounds? Do we look at that in terms of the amount of recruits we have from different groups? ... How are we going to measure the way that we are improving relations ... with a group say like Irish Travellers who really aren't up at the top of the pile? ... The main prioritisation ... with race relations [RRAA 2001] is going to [the] Asian community, because the community development officers ... are predominantly Asian. ... It takes something [like] "nine-eleven" [or] September [19]81 in London to a lesser degree with the riots there - and politics becomes

involved. ... Are we looking at inclusion or just making sure that we are safe and
we've got the right intelligence? ... I guess ... there is not really the political
drive to look at the Irish community ... so therefore Travellers [are] not a
priority.

Sivanandan (cited in Whyte, 2002: 40) sums up the real dilemma for the state
and its institutions in the post MacPherson period:

/It] is the state which – through its laws and its edicts, its administration of the
public services - sets the tone and the tenor, the climate, of race relations in
society. By refusing, therefore, to examine and outlaw racism in its own
structures, the state gives a fillip to popular racism and embeds it in popular
culture. Since public officers such as the police are drawn from that society and
culture, the virus of racism is carried back into the body politic. State racism
contaminates civil society.

Again, the responsibility returns onto the state and its institutions. Government,
from the top down, must take responsibility for the implementation of policy
and associated legislation that protects ethnic minorities from racism and
discrimination instead of taking a pragmatic and selective approach that de-
legitimises ethnic groups like the Irish Travellers.   Similarly the state's
contradictory attitude to Irish Travellers encourages the virus of anti-Traveller
racism throughout society as a whole. Whilst affording them ethnic recognition
in law, they are simultaneously criminalised by the legislative assembly and
persecuted by elements of the state through institutions like the police.

Conclusion

The state has a responsibility to challenge anti-Traveller racism within its
institutions including the police.   Aspects of criminal law (for instance the
CJPOA 1994) discriminate against Travellers culture and lifestyle in the context
of the Human Rights Act (1998) and the RRAA (2001) and should be amended
or abolished as they have created an 'outlaw' community and intensified the
forced assimilation of Irish Travellers into settled accommodation. The cultural
breakdown that has resulted from these policies has undoubtedly led to a
degradation of Irish Travellers' social and cultural bulwarks such as the
extended family and traditional economies, thereby leading to the social
alienation and criminalisation of young Irish Travellers. Media reporting of
stories about Travellers have usually reinforced negative stereotypes and these
are exacerbated by opportunistic and ill-informed statements by (often senior)
politicians that further alienate Irish Travellers.

Many police forces have been reluctant to use the draconian anti-Traveller measures as set up in the CJPOA (1994). Diversity-led initiatives to combat negative stereotypes and improve service delivery to Travellers by some police forces in the wake of the Macpherson Report (1999) recommendations have produced some interesting material. However these outcomes have not had any direct influence or input into Public Order policy as relating to crucial issues such as the protocols on illegal encampments. The remit of TLOs is essentially based around public order concerns and the exact nature of their deployment is delegated to local police commanders, thus undermining a more comprehensive and culturally-sensitive policing approach to Traveller-related issues. Independent Advisory Groups set up to improve relations between ethnic minorities and the police have produced little positive policy change for Irish Travellers or other culturally nomadic groups and are seen as unrepresentative 'talking shops' by many critics, while 'third party reporting' initiatives for Travellers have not materialised either. Evidence from a number of police forces also indicates that PACE 'stop and search' powers are used disproportionately against Travellers.

Strengthening police powers almost begets abuse. Macpherson's refusal to limit the power that PACE (1984) and police discretion permitted, meant that his Report reinforced by default the legitimacy of police stop-and-search powers. Thus, the Macpherson Report (1999) can be viewed as a hegemonic rebuilding process following the Lawrence murder and the institutional repercussions that came in its aftermath. Another by-product of Macpherson is its affirmation of the unbalanced targeting of some ethnic minority communities. Whyte (2002: 40) asserts that: 'In this sphere [particularly regarding stop and search powers], Macpherson has played a central role in the reproduction of discriminatory practices that are embedded in police work'. Even more worrying are the instances recorded above of unofficial memorandums sent by local police management to residents and local services labelling newly-arrived nomadic Travellers as the main source of petty crime in local communities.

New community-policing initiatives that emphasise an actuarial approach and target 'at risk' youth in schools and youth clubs will miss many young Irish Travellers - both 'settled' and nomadic - whose kinship ties are much more important than links with sedentary communities and associated services. Linked to the failures in community policing as relating to Irish Travellers are major problems in how diversity training has been 'packaged' and delivered to the police. Diversity training in police forces has been under-resourced and very little attention has been paid to challenging concepts such as the black/white binary and (more specifically) - the sensitivities and living situations of white or culturally nomadic minorities like Irish Travellers. Some police trainers identify the concept of 'Irishness' as having very negative connotations in some British police forces and acknowledge that there is widespread and overt police racism directed at Irish Travellers both in training and operationally. In light of the recent Morris Enquiry Report (2004), exposing internal racism in the MPS and the shocking overt racism displayed in the 'Secret Policeman' (http://www.blink.org.uk/docs/secret_policeman.htm) television documentary by some new recruits in a number of English police forces, the MENC police management response to the publication of the 'Room to Roam' report was to identify who Sergeant Plummer was – (from the text) - and to informally discipline him in relation to quotations attributed to him in the research report. MENC police have never responded publicly or privately to the author in relation to any of the 'Room to Roam' Report's allegations or recommendations about their treatment of Irish Travellers. Clearly, despite repeated investigations and reports many issues still remain to be addressed by police forces in Britain as regards policing ethnicity in an equitable and culturally-sensitive manner – most notably as relating to culturally nomadic groups generally and Irish Travellers in particular.

References

Acton, T (1994) 'Categorising Irish Travellers', in M. McCann et al, Irish Travellers: Culture and Ethnicity, Belfast: Queen's Universitym, 36-53.

Chatterton, M (1993). "Rational Management in Police Organisations: A Comparative Study in Two Forces." Unpublished paper.

Clements, L and Smith, P (1997) *Traveller Law Reform: TLAST/TLRU conference and consultation report*. Cardiff: TLAST & TLRU.

GUARDIAN: London based national newspaper.

Her Majesty's Inspectorate of Constabulary (1999) *Winning the Race: Policing Plural Communities Revisited*, London: Home Office.

Hickman, M and Walter, B (1997) *Discrimination and the Irish Community in Britain*. London: CRE.

Hillyard, P (1993) *Suspect Community: People's Experience of the Prevention of Terrorism Act in Britain*, London: Pluto Press.

Home Office (1997). *Race and The Criminal Justice System*. London: Home Office.

Macpherson, W (1999) *The Stephen Lawrence Inquiry*, Cm 4262. London: Stationery Office.

McCann, M., Ó Síocháin, S. and Ruane, J. (eds) (1994) *Irish Travellers: Culture and Ethnicity*. Belfast: Queen's University.

McCarthy, P (1994) 'The sub-culture of poverty reconsidered', M. McCann et al (eds.) *Irish Travellers: culture and ethnicity*, Belfast: The Institute of Irish Studies, The Queen's University of Belfast.

McConville, M et al (1991) *The Case for The Prosecution: police suspects and the construction of criminality*, London: Routledge.

McLaughlin, E (25 January 2000) 'The Racialisation of Community in Crime Control Discourses', paper presented to *Rethinking Crime Prevention and Community Safety, a seminar*. The Open University.

Morris Inquiry (2004) *The Case for Change, The Report of the The Morris Inquiry*. London: Metropolitan Police Service.

Morris, R and Clements, L (eds) (1999*). Gaining Ground: Law Reform for Gypsies and Travellers*. Hatfield: University of Hertfordshire Press.

O'Flynn, J (July 1993) *Identity Crisis, Access to Social Security and ID Ch*ecks. London: Action Group for Irish Youth.

Parekh Report (2000) *The Future of Multi-Ethnic Britain*. Report of the Runnymede Trust Commission on the future of multi-ethnic Britain. London: Profile Books Ltd.

Power, C. (2004) *Room to Roam: England's Irish Travellers - a Report of Research*, London: Community Fund.

—. (2003) Irish Travellers: Ethnicity, Racism, and PSRs, *Probation Journal*, Vol. 50, September Issue 03.

Reiner, R 1992, *The Politics of the Police*. (2nd edn), Toronto: University of Toronto Press.

Scarman Report (1981) *The Brixton Disorders 10-12 April 1981*, Cmnd 8427, London: Her Majesty's Stationary Office.

Secret Policeman television documentary (BBC) transcript accessed on 24 February 2006 http://www.blink.org.uk/docs/secret_policeman.htm

Sharpe, J (1983) *Crime in Seventeenth Century England: A County Study*. Cambridge: University Press.

Sibley, D (1995) *Geographies of Exclusion – Societies and Difference in the West*. London: Routledge.

Whyte, D (2002), *Contextualising Police Racism: the aftermath of the MacPherson Report and the local response on Merseyside*, Centre for Criminal Justice Occasional Paper 2, Liverpool: Liverpool John Moores University.

CHAPTER NINE

POLICING GYPSIES AND TRAVELLERS

DR JOANNA RICHARDSON,
CENTRE FOR COMPARATIVE HOUSING RESEARCH,
DE MONTFORT UNIVERSITY, LEICESTER

This essay examines some aspects of the way in which Gypsies and Travellers are 'policed' in British society, a process of "policing" which is discussed in the widest sense of the word. Travellers and Gypsies are groups which are acknowledged as being subject to increased societal surveillance as a consequence of their status as 'other' or 'deviant'. Media discourse, by the public and politicians serves to socially construct the deviant Gypsy/Traveller and there is much current debate on 'controlling' the 'influx' and 'invasion' of public spaces. The aim of this essay is to examine some of the wider issues around policing Gypsies and Travellers, and to introduce areas of good practice. This is debated within a theoretical context of control and power, and specifically draws upon the work of Foucault. This discussion is constructed within a frame of reference where the term "policing" encompasses the surveillance of Traveller and Gypsy communities on the wider societal level by the "majority" or non-Traveller community.

Introduction

Almost 40 years ago I watched police officers deliberately kick burning sticks onto children to force the Travellers to move on quickly. Ways to move them have become less crude but equally effective. They depend, it seems to me, on utter and total prejudice and ignorance in almost the whole of our society.
—Dawson, 2000: 4

Dawson outlines his views of the treatment of Gypsies and Travellers, by the police and others, and suggests that there should be more understanding and toleration in our diverse community, particularly as a consequence of the Macpherson Report (1999). This chapter examines how Gypsies and Travellers in Britain are 'policed' both in the wider sense of being under the control and surveillance of society; and in a more narrow and defined sense i.e. how they are treated by the police, particularly as regards the issue of unauthorised encampments.

Traditionally, the definition of Gypsies and Travellers has been difficult. It must be noted that, under the Race Relations Act (1976) and subsequent case law (CRE v Dutton, 1989 and O'Leary and others v Punch Retail, 2000), Gypsies and Travellers are recognised minority groups. Prior to this, the focus has primarily been on the nomadism of Gypsies and Travellers, as part of any legal definition. However, the Office of the Deputy Prime Minister has recently recognised the difficulties concerning the concept of 'settled' Travellers; and as part of its consultation on updating Circular 1/94 has mooted the following definition:

> For the purposes of this Circular "Gypsies and Travellers" means
>
> *A person or persons who have a traditional cultural preference for living in caravans and who either pursue a nomadic habit of life or have pursued such a habit but have ceased travelling, whether permanently or temporarily, because of the education needs of their dependent children, or ill-health, old age, or caring responsibilities (whether of themselves, their dependants living with them, or the widows and widowers of such dependents), but does not include members of an organised group of travelling show people or circus people, travelling together as such.*
>
> (Planning for Gypsy and Traveller Sites, Consultation Paper, 2004: 11)

Two other terms which may need clarification for the purposes of this essay are 'Gaujo/gorgia' – the Gypsy word for a non-Gypsy – and 'gavver' – the Gypsy word for police.

The legislation concerning Gypsies and Travellers is extensive. For instance, the Anti-Social Behaviour Act (2003) Section 62 allows police to move Gypsies and Travellers on from unauthorised sites where a council plot is available. Also there is the Planning and Compulsory Purchase Act (2004), and Circular (02/2005) which was published in March 2005 and which gave guidance on Temporary Stop Notices – (allowed for in Part Four of the Act) - on unauthorised developments. Political and legislative debate continues regarding the Criminal Justice and Public Order Act (1994) which removed the duty on local authorities to provide Gypsy/Traveller sites. Section 61 of this Act permitted the police to request trespassers on private land to leave immediately.

The Office of the Deputy Prime Minister (ODPM) Planning, Local Government and the Regions Select Committee published their report in November 2004, calling for the duty of site provision on the part of Local Authorities to be reinstated. The response in early 2005 was that the Government did not feel that a duty was needed. However, ODPM have still asked councils to provide extra sites, in their good practice guide *Diversity in Equality and Planning* (March 2005). Commentators suggest this will not be possible without enforcing a duty (Hilditch, 2005). Additionally, local authorities should also adhere to the Homelessness Act (2002) which requires them to carry out homelessness reviews and to formulate and publish strategies; plus the Housing Act (2004) includes Section 225 which places a specific duty on local authorities to assess the accommodation needs of Gypsies and Travellers. The ODPM has already reprimanded one council in Brentwood (Inside Housing, 2005: 6), for not including the needs of this group in their local development plans, as required by the Planning and Compulsory Purchase Act (2004). There is a suggestion that not providing sites for Travellers can be as costly as getting on with provision (Morris and Clements, 2002) and there has been examination of how the police and wider legislation affects Gypsies and Travellers (Morris, 2001 and O'Nions, 1995). There is an agenda for dealing with Gypsies and Travellers – new powers to evict and to stop unauthorised development of sites; in anticipation of new local authority sites being built. It is in this context that the policing of Gypsies and Travellers, particularly on unauthorised encampments, takes place.

Theoretical Context of Control

This chapter focuses on the surveillant control of a minority (Gypsies and Travellers) by the majority of society. As a tool of that majority, the police overtly control Gypsies and Travellers; but before moving onto that it is interesting to outline the more covert type of control in wider society. This more covert type of surveillance can be seen in the context of a framework of control and power. Dandeker (1990) helps to clarify a typology of surveillance, with five main types: (1) Petty Tyranny, (2) Direct Democracy, (3) Patronage, (4) Bureaucratic Dictatorship, (5) Rational-Legal (see Figure 1).

Fig. 1 Typology of surveillance, adapted from Dandeker, 1990: 45-51

	Personal Administration		**Bureaucratic Administration**
Autocratic Interests	*Petty Tyranny* Autocratic power is exercised over a subject population by a single person whose means of supervision and information gathering do not extend much beyond his or her own personal capacities.		*Bureaucratic Dictatorship* Personalism and competition pervade the system, factionalism operates in such a way that the ruler cannot relate to the bureaucracy as if it were a dependable administrative machine.
		Patronage Surveillance activities and the reproduction of systems of rule are tenuous social processes characterised by personalism as well as the anonymous or impersonal features more prevalent in modern societies. Surveillance activities are autonomous from controls of the subject population and of bureaucratic discipline.	

Liberal Interests	*Direct Democracy* Surveillance activities are carried out by all members of the collectivity in pursuit of popular interests, although this may result in the tyranny of the majority over the liberties of particular individuals or minorities.		*Rational-Legal* Both ruler and bureaucracy are accountable effectively to the subject population and distributive resources according to a widely held ethic of acceptable bureaucratic behaviour.

'Direct Democracy' and 'Gaze'

This chapter is most interested in the type of surveillance that Dandeker (1990) refers to as 'Direct Democracy'. He says that this involves the "...tyranny of the majority over the liberties of particular individuals or minorities." Foucault's (1969) 'gaze' might help to explain more about this 'tyranny of the majority' through their surveillant control of the minority who don't conform to societal norms.

Foucault's 'gaze' might best be described as the eye of power and control. In *The Birth of the Clinic* Foucault describes gaze, thus:

> ...the gaze is not faithful to truth, nor subject to it, without asserting, at the same time, a supreme mastery: the gaze that sees is a gaze that dominates.
> —Foucault, 1969: 39

Foucault believed that the gaze was not only exemplified in the panopticon of Bentham's 18th Century prison designs, but could be extended, through institutions, to the wider society.

> ...the best way of managing prisoners was to make them the potential targets of the authority's gaze at every moment of the day. And this authoritative gaze didn't reside in a particular person, rather it was recognised as part of the system, a way of looking that could operate as a general principle of surveillance throughout the social body. This logic of the gaze, like that of discipline, was not confined to the prison, but moved throughout the various institutional spaces in society.
> —Danaher *et al.* 2000: 54

The crucial element in the gaze is the interpretive element. Foucault (1969) was discussing it in relation to doctors looking at illnesses in their patients. He explained that doctors no longer passively viewed symptoms, but instead started to actively interpret them. The gaze is not passive surveillance, but active interpretation and domination. It is suggested that this is also true of discourse. Words and terms used in the discourse around Gypsies and Travellers are not passively describing a situation but instead they are interpreting them. The interpretation involved in discourse is based on a variety of variables including the ontology of the speaker and their social norms and characteristics.

It is important to remember though, that gaze is not a uni-directional process. It should be understood within a relational concept of power.

> Power is employed and exercised through a net-like organisation. And not only do individuals circulate between its threads; they are always in the position of simultaneously undergoing and exercising this power. They are not only its inert or consenting target; they are always also the elements of its articulation. In other words, individuals are the vehicles of power, not its point of application.
> —Foucault, 1980: 98

The 'target' population is also a 'vehicle of power' according to the Foucaultian definition. An example of this relational type of power and surveillant control is found in the Gypsy Traveller Media Advisory Group, which was established in 2003 by representatives of the travelling community. The aim was to monitor the media representation and, where appropriate, take action such as meet with broadcasters and journalists, or report issues to the Commission for Racial Equality. This group personifies the relational power that Foucault discusses; those who are under surveillance from the media are now monitoring the media (see Richardson, forthcoming 2006).

It is important to remember that the gaze is a metaphor, but it is a useful explanation of surveillance at work in society as a tool of control. McNay (1994) discusses this different perception of power and control:

> Control in modern societies is achieved, therefore, not through direct repression but through more invisible strategies of normalization. Individuals regulate themselves through a constant introspective search for their hidden 'truth', held to lie in their innermost identity.
> —McNay, 1994: 97

Surveillance of different people in society can be rooted in different motives. Lyon (2002) sees that motives may have changed over ages:

But what is all this 'watching' for? This too, is in flux. Once, police kept an eye on a specific person, suspected for some good reason of an offence. Or the debt collector tried to track down defaulters who owed money to others. While such practices still occur, much more likely is the creation of categories of interest and classes of conduct thought worthy of attention. If the modern world displayed an urge to classify, today this urge is endemic in surveillance systems... to capture personal data triggered by human bodies and to use these abstractions to place people in new social classes of income, attributes, habits, preferences, or offences, in order to influence, manage, or control them.
—Lyon, 2002: 3

It would appear, then, that surveillance is not just about controlling those who are seen to be 'deviant' in society. Instead it is about gathering enough intelligence about minority groups in order to be able to label them in the first place. Lyon's understanding of the motive for surveillance, today, in society, seems to echo the notion of Foucault's (1969) gaze; in that intelligence gathering is not just about objective facts. It is about interpreting those facts in order to label people as 'deviant', much as the doctors, that Foucault studied, interpreted symptoms of ill patients to make a diagnosis.

'Society' and Folk-Devils

It is difficult to know who is doing the watching and who is under surveillance; especially as power is so fluid and can be changing all the time. However, to make sensible progress with a debate an assumption has to be made. Society as a whole, including institutions such as the government and the police, forms an apparatus of control and surveillance. The motive for surveillance is to label people thought to be deviant, in order to say to the rest of society 'this is how not to behave, these people do not live according to our accepted macro norms'. A variety of minority groups have been labelled as 'other' or 'deviant'; examples include young single mothers, asylum seekers and Gypsies and Travellers. In addition it is possible to suggest that in raising the profile of 'deviant' minority groups the government can raise the levels of fear and panic and this can allow policy and legislative shifts that would otherwise not be acquiesced by the public or opposition politicians. One can see examples of significant policy and legislative shifts in the terrorism laws introduced post 9/11.

Cohen (1980) examined the notions of moral panics and folk devils. His work argues that the use of moral panics has become more sophisticated since his case study of the Mods and the Rockers. He states that the old sequence, where a specific event triggered a panic, a moral enterprise - followed by mobilisation of control culture - is now gone. In its place a general sense of disquiet is created:

> The control culture is mobilized in advance, real events being anticipated and taken to confirm and justify the need for gradual ideological repression.
> —Cohen, 1980: xxiv

This theory does take a rather sinister and negative view of the state's role in the creation and use of moral panics. The use of state control is necessary in an orderly society; the entire premise of the social contract (Rousseau, 1994) is that in 'opting in' to society one agrees to adhere to the rules, which will better life for the majority of society. This 'social contract' concept has been discussed recently by Miliband (2005):

> What do I mean by social contract? I mean shared expectations of what citizens will do for themselves and for each other, and shared understanding about what they can expect from government. Shared expectations that embody moral commitments and common values. Shared expectations that unite self interest and common interest.
> —Miliband, 2005: 2

Miliband may feel that he has updated an old idea, but the shared expectations and common values are of the 'majority' and do not necessarily include 'others' such as Gypsies and Travellers; and so laudable aims to break down old power hierarchies in a new social contract, may be viewed as a touch gauche. Cohen's (1980) moral panics theory sees governments shaping and controlling behaviour in order to retain and increase their power.

Folk devils are the focus of moral panics. In Cohen's study, which took place in the 1960's and 1970's, these were groups of 'youth' – Mods and Rockers. Cohen helps to describe the term folk devil:

> But the groups such as the Teddy Boys and the Mods and Rockers have been distinctive in being identified not just in terms of particular events (such as demonstrations) or particular disapproved forms of behaviour (such as drug-taking or violence) but as distinguishable social types.
> —Cohen, 1980: 9

Therefore, the folk devil is not necessarily seen in context of a type of behaviour. Instead, some group members may have helped to define the group but then the media/society/state define the whole group as a particular social type.

There is a plethora of folk devils that goes beyond Cohen's case study; for example Gypsies. In old-wives' tales Gypsies stole babies; according to Anne Widdecombe they steal pets (see Turner, 2002) and according to people in a local planning consultation exercise, they are murderers (see Richardson, forthcoming, 2006). The role of Gypsies and Travellers as folk devils is played out in government policy decisions and is reinforced by the media. The government, for instance, uses the role of Gypsy as folk devil from a functionalist perspective in order to tell the rest of society how not to live.

The theory of proximity (Bauman, 1989) is important in understanding folk devils of all kinds, from asylum seekers to Gypsies. He suggests that the more 'other' people are made to seem, the less the rest of society cares about their treatment; this theory was proposed in relation to the treatment of Jews in the Second World War, by the Nazis. Bauman (1989) explains the importance of proximity:

> Being inextricably tied to human proximity, morality seems to conform to the law of optical perspective. It looms large and thick close to the eye. With the growth of distance, responsibility for the other shrivels, moral dimensions of the object blur, till both reach the vanishing point and disappear from view.
> —Bauman, 1989: 192

For Gypsies and Travellers, this law of proximity can be seen to work. Gypsies can be 'moved on' after 28 days, according to the Criminal Justice and Public Order Act (1994). They are not allowed to 'settle' on certain unauthorised sites and yet there are not enough authorised sites to accommodate them, and they are not given planning permission to build their own sites either. This bureaucracy is effective in maintaining a distance between 'us' and 'them'. The distance allows society to believe they are not like 'us' and its conscience remains clear when Gypsies and Travellers are treated badly either by the public, the press, the police or the government. The distance created between Gypsies and 'us' has allowed them to become folk devils, and allows them to be treated differently without too much introspection and troubled conscience.

The theme of 'folk devils' was evident during primary research undertaken for another study (see Richardson, forthcoming, 2006). During a conversation with an officer from a local authority undergoing a planning consultation, the image of Gypsies and Travellers as 'other', as folk devils, was discussed:

> Interestingly, if you talk to people today there are a lot of urban myths of how bad the Travellers were, from murders to eating people's pets. At the time however, very few complaints were raised. Without a doubt the criticism of Travellers has grown over the intervening years.

—Planning Officer, 2004

Many of the stories in the media, or conversations amongst the public, are about the folk-devil Gypsy and there are pressures on local authorities, housing associations and the police to 'deal with the problem'. There hasn't actually been a huge rise in unauthorised encampments, according to official figures from the Office of the Deputy Prime Minister (ODPM), but there is a public perception that such an issue is on the increase. The count of Gypsy caravans, undertaken by ODPM, is recognised to be in need of improvement (Niner, 2004); however their figures for the bi-annual count show that for January 2003 there were 3028 caravans on unauthorised encampments, in January 2004, there were 3571 and in January 2005 there were 3558; so in fact there were less caravans in January 2005, than in 2004. Regardless of the official figures, there is a perception that unauthorised encampments are on the increase and that this is causing raised tensions in local communities. The prevalence of such perceptions, perceptions which frequently have no real basis in fact, are an exemplar of that construct which the various theorists have termed "gaze". As discussed in this essay – it is the "gaze", that often-imperceptive form of policing that is the surveillance of society's "Others" which serves to socially construct and monitor Travellers and Gypsies as a so-called "deviant" group in modern Britain.

References

Anti-Social Behaviour Act 2003, London, HMSO, accessed through www.hmso.gov.uk/acts/acts2003/30038--h.htm on April 24th 2004.

Bauman, Z (1989) *Modernity and the Holocaust*, Oxford: Polity Press.

BBC Inside Out (2005) *Unrest on Council Gypsy Sites*, www.bbc.co.uk/insideout/south/series7/gypsies.shtml accessed 05/07/05.

Bowers, J. (2004) Against all odds, *Travellers Times*, Issue 19, Spring 2004.

—. (undated) *Prejudice and Pride: The Experiences of Young Travellers in Cambridgeshire*, Cambridgeshire: Ormiston Children and Families Trust.

Census 2001, www.statistics.gov.uk/census

Cohen, S. (1980) *Folk Devils and Moral Panics, The Creation of the Mods and Rockers*, Oxford: Martin Robertson.

Coxhead, J. (2004) *Anti-Racism Training Strategies for the Police Service and Criminal Justice Sector, Gypsies and Travellers*, Derbyshire Police Service

—. (2005 forthcoming) *'Moving Forward' How the Gypsy and Traveller Communities can be more engaged to improve policing performance*, London: The Home Office.

CRE v Dutton (1989) 1 AllER 306.

Danaher, G. Schirato, T. and Webb, J. (2000) *Understanding Foucault*, London: Sage.

Dandeker, C. (1990) *Surveillance, Power & Modernity*, London: Polity Press.

Dawson, R. (2000) *Crime and Prejudice: Traditional Travellers*, Derbyshire: Robert Dawson.

Dodd, V. (2005) "Met chief: my critics will not stop me", *The Guardian*, 2nd July 2005, pg 1.

Foucault, M. (1969) *The Birth of the Clinic: An Archaeology of Medical Perception*, translated by A.M Sheridan, London: Tavistock Publications.

—. (1980) *Power/ Knowledge* edited by Colin Gordon, Harlow: Pearson Education Ltd.

Garland, D. (2001) *The Culture of Control – crime and social order in contemporary society*, Oxford: Oxford University Press.

Gil-Robles, A. (2005) *Report by Mr Alvaro Gil-Robles, Commissioner for Human Rights, on his visit to the United Kingdom, 4th-12th November, 2004* www.libertysecurity.org/article268.html accessed 1st July 2005.

Hilditich, M. (2005) ODPM takes Gypsies and Travellers' side in sites row, *Housing Today*, 11th March, Pg 9.

Homelessness Act 2002, London: HMSO.

Housing Act 2004, London: The Stationery Office.

Inside Housing (2005) 'Government set to use new gypsy land powers', *Inside Housing*, 11th March, pg 6.

London Borough of Newham (2003) *Report to the Mayor – Unauthorised Encampments and Associated Illegal Activity*, London: LB Newham.

Lyon, D. (2002) Editorial.   Surveillance Studies: Understanding visibility, mobility and the phenetic fix, *Surveillance and Society*, Vol. 1, No. 1, Pgs 1-7.

McNay, L. (1994) *Foucault a critical introduction* Cambridge: Polity Press.

Miliband, D. (2005) *Building a Modern Social Contract*, speech to the 'Together we Can' conference, accessed via www.odpm.gov.uk on 11th August 2005.

Milton Keynes Citizens' Advisory Group on Travellers, *Report*, 24 March, 1999.

Milton Keynes Council, *Joint Planning Forum on Travellers, Traveller Strategy*, undated.

Milton Keynes Council, *Policy on Unauthorised Encampments*, undated.

Morris, R. (2001) Gypsies and Travellers: new policies, new approaches, *Police Research and Management*, Vol 5, No. 1, Pgs 41-49.

Morris, R. and Clements, L. (2002) *At What Cost? The economics of Gypsy and Traveller encampments*, Bristol: Policy Press.

O'Nions, H. (1995) *The Marginalisation of Gypsies*, University of Leicester http://webjcli.ncl.ac.uk/articles3/onions3.html accessed 23/03/04.

Observer (2004) *Gypsy Camp Plea by Police to Deter Racist Thugs*, www.romnews.com/community/modules.php accessed on 19th July 2005

Office of the Deputy Prime Minister (2004) *Guidance on Managing Unauthorised Camping*, London: ODPM.

—. (2004) *Planning for Gypsy and Traveller Sites, Consultation Paper*, London: ODPM.

—. (2005) *Count of gypsy caravans on 19th January 2005, last five counts*, London: ODPM.

Planning and Compulsory Purchase Act (2004) London: House of Commons

Randall, B. (2005) 'Local Hero', *Communities Today*, 3rd August, 2005, pgs 16-18.

Richardson, J. (2004) *Talking about Gypsies: the notion of discourse as control*, PhD thesis, Leicester: De Montfort University.

Rose, D. (2005) "Mission: protect the weak", *The Observer*, 3rd July, 2005, pg 15.

Society Guardian (2005) *Council creates no-go zones for travellers*, http://society.guardian.co.uk accessed 31/05/05

Taggart, I. (undated) *Gypsy Travellers A Policing Strategy*, Grampian Police.

This is Basildon (2005) *Campaign taken to the UN*, www.thisisbasildon.co.uk/essex/basildon/news accessed 02/08/05

Travellers' Times (2005) *Traveller law 'unworkable' say police*, Travellers Times, Issue 24, pg 1.

Williams, N. (2004) *Gypsy and Traveller Matter, The Metropolitan Police Service Policy on Engagement with Travelling People*, London: MPS

—. (undated) *The Customs of Travelling People – A Guide to working with the Travelling Community*, London: Metropolitan Police Authority.

CHAPTER TEN

SHELTA AND VERLAN: 'OUTSIDERS' TALKING BACK

ST. JOHN Ó DONNABHÁIN

Introduction

This essay explores a number of similarities between the linguistic structure and functions of two languages as spoken by so-called "outsider" societal groups – Shelta as spoken by the Irish Traveller community in Ireland and abroad and Verlan, the language or linguistic register used today in France, principally by the "alienated" youth in the banlieues (suburbs) of many major French cities, many of whom are today of either Arab or African origin. It also examines the societal implications of the status of the Shelta and Verlan, and the interconnection between language and society at large.

As a fluent speaker of Irish and French, my first reaction upon encountering the Irish Traveller language Shelta (the academic term for what is commonly referred to as Cant or Gammon), was to notice some immediately obvious similarities with the French language game Verlan, not least what has been termed the 'backslang' common to them both, i.e. *cailín* (girl) becomes *laicín* in Shelta[1]; *femme* (woman or wife) becomes *meuf* in Verlan[2]. Interest thus piqued, I set out to explore if this was simply happenstance, or if there were meaningful parallels to be drawn between the two. This discussion will be structured around an examination of the commonalities in structuring, and the changes made in both Shelta and Verlan. This will then be extrapolated to look at the

---

[1] Alice Binchy, 'Traveller's Language: A Sociolinguistic Perspective' in McCann, May, Ó Síocháin, Séamus and Ruane, Joseph (eds.), *Irish Travellers: Culture and Ethnicity* (Belfast, 1994), p.135

[2] John Henley, 'Try to be on-line, but don't be a hamster' *The Guardian* [online] 4 January 2003. http://www.guardian.co.uk/france/story/0,,868543,00.html (11 April 2006).

implications in terms of the 'outsider' status of Irish Travellers and of France's 'Beurs' (Verlanised 'Arabe'; a common term for second- or third-generation immigrants from the Maghreb or North Africa) and the group identity which is involved in the language and its use. These will seek to explore the comparability of Shelta and Verlan, and what we can learn through their commonalities and differences.

As mentioned above, the most immediately apparent trait that Shelta and Verlan share is in their method of inverting some words, which can have the function of rendering them gibberish to the untrained ear – both of them are almost exclusively orally communicated, lacking an independent grammar (both use the grammar of the dominant form – English and French respectively). Ó Baoill points to the fact that 'the form in which [the non-English lexicon] of Cant was acquired from Irish gives Cant its particular synchronic colouring'. He styles Cant a 'register', and points to phrases such as *ód niucs (dó ceann)* or 'two pennies'; *losped (pós + '-ed')* or 'married', as examples of how numerous Cant words are constructed[3]. A similar structure can be seen in Verlan – indeed the word 'Verlan' comes from when *l'inverse* (the opposite, backwards) is itself inverted, and then spelled phonetically. This metathesis can be enacted on many words, such as *ziquemu (musique* or 'music'); *chébran (branché* or 'plugged-in' i.e. cool) or *keuf (flic* or 'cop')[4].

This final example of *keuf* is a good example, with its loss of the letter 'l' as part of the process of work manipulation; *cena (teach* or 'house') sees a comparable loss of the 't'[5]. *Grandy,* which is the Irish-American Traveller word for 'candy', with an arbitrary prefix added, is an example of importation from English[6]; this also takes place in Verlan, with languages such as Arabic contributing words such as *kif,* meaning (variously) 'well-being', 'to fancy' or 'to like a lot' (in verb form), and in the phrase *kif-kif demain* – 'same shit, different day'[7]. While these similarities are not wholesale, and there are many characteristics in both Shelta and Verlan without parallel in the other (such as around the scale of use, claims to language status and so on), there are also undoubtedly also strong grounds for comparison and examination of the

[3] Dónall P. Ó Baoill, 'Travellers' Cant – Language or Register' in McCann, May, Ó Síocháin, Séamus and Ruane, Joseph (eds.), *Irish Travellers: Culture and Ethnicity* (Belfast, 1994), p.159.
[4] Natalie J. Lefkowitz, '*Verlan*: Talking backwards in French', *French Review,* 63 (1989), pp.314-16.
[5] Míchéal Ó hAodha, 'Travellers' Language: Some Irish Language perspectives' in Kirk, John M. and Ó Baoill, Dónall P. (eds.), *Travellers and their Language* (Belfast, 2002).
[6] Ó Baoill, 'Travellers' Cant', p.161.
[7] Fazia Guene, 'Back to the Streets' *The Guardian* [online] 24 December 2005. http://books.guardian.co.uk/comment/story/0,,1673488,00.html (10 April 2006).

commonalities which link these two forms of speech, and the people who speak them.

Use by a marginalised group

The 'outsider' status of Travellers in Ireland and Beurs in France offers an interesting lens through which to examine the use of Shelta and Verlan. Both groups are placed on the outside looking in at their respective dominant societies. The ideology of sedentarism marginalises those who do not conform to ideas of personal private property, and seeks to eradicate nomads by overtaking their space and criminalising them[8]. This representation of the 'Other' – neither the same nor totally different (therein lies the discomfort) onto whom one, or a society at large, can project their misdeeds and insecurities is held in common with the positioning of Beurs in France. These predominantly young people living on the margins of cities, in the poorest areas (another thing they share with Travellers) have little in terms of amenities or prospects. The riots of suburbs such as Clichy-sous-Bois which rocked France last year were a response to these dead-end circumstances, but also to the widespread blaming of all of France's problems on them, mainly by the media and the better-off in society[9]. This racialisation and projection of ills onto the powerless and marginalised – Beurs are a small minority of the population, while Travellers make up less than 1% of Ireland's inhabitants – serves to limit their ability to be part of society, by delegitimising them and the fact that they're non-mainstream. Verlan and Shelta are affected by this.

In these cases, reassertion of identity through language in the face of colonisation is an experience familiar to both. This is quite straightforward in the French case, insofar as it fits snugly in with the post-colonial context and power relations which characterise the relationship between the Beurs and 'mainstream' French society[10]. On the other hand, in the Irish context, the colonised becomes the coloniser when Catholic, rural, conservative, land-obsessed nationalism becomes hegemonic, and then seeks to expel the difference which Travellers represent. Language thus becomes a cultural marker whose value, or lack thereof, is a matter of dispute between the various sections of society, dominant versus subordinate.

---

[8] Robbie McVeigh, 'Theorising sedentarism' in Acton, T.A (ed.), *Gypsy Politics and Traveller Identity* (Hatfield, England: 1997), pp.22-24.
[9] Alex Duval Smith, 'Playing with Fire' *The Observer* [online] 5 February 2006. http://www.guardian.co.uk/france/story/0,,1702321,00.html (9 April 2006).
[10] Alec G. Hargreaves, 'Resistance and Identity in Beur Narratives', *Modern Fiction Studies*, 35 (1989), p.91.

The legitimacy of Shelta and Verlan amounts to a power struggle between these sections of society over the control of language. Dominant society uses education to inculcate its values, as seen in the (in)famous French examples of the textbook which begins with the phrase 'Our ancestors the Gauls'[11]. This functions also through the definition of what language in 'acceptable' – this is the manner in which a certain type of language use becomes culturally exalted. Discourses of 'purity' of language also contributed to these types of attitudes. Argot is delegitmised in this fashion, keeping power for those who speak 'correctly'. Binchy notes the importance of the status of a language when she explores how Shelta is concealed (at least partly) because of the internalisation of negative dominant societal attitudes by Travellers. Shelta is perceived as deviant, and consequently, its only use is seen to be 'against' settled people[12]. These problems are exacerbated, in the case of both Shelta and Verlan, by the overbearing influence of another, overriding, language – of Gaeilge and English over the former, and of French over the latter.   By comparison with these long-established languages, natural practices of borrowing, seen in all lexicons and attributable to proximity, have often lead to their delegitimation as not 'real' languages.

This is intimately connected to the marginalised position in society which both Travellers and Beurs occupy. As 'outsiders', their culture and ways of life are seen as having little merit – as are their languages. And given that these languages are themselves denigrated, a process of double- feedback ensues, which reinforces this subordinated position. The inevitability of this sequence is readily apparent, and the separation between the 'haves' and the 'have-nots' leads in tern to a search for new sources of pride and value among the debris of that belittled by dominant society. But this seeming rendering of Travellers and Beurs as powerless is in its turn reinterpreted by these subordinated groups as a language through which to express themselves in a subversive fashion. Power relations are fundamentally altered by this act of resistance, which renders contestable supposedly fixed notions of value in society, and introduces a whole new realm of powerful identification into this equation. This process will be explored further later in this work.

Secrecy and communication

The disguise function of the language game Verlan can be seen as a centrally important facet of its use. Hargreaves observes how it 'fractures normal

---

[11] Hargreaves, 'Resistance and Identity' p.95.
[12] Binchy, 'Travellers Language', pp.143-44.

communicative process'[13] as a centrally important part of the argot and slang of
the disenfranchised in present day France. The association of this group with
crime (which marginalisation can often lead to) sees 'word clusters' or a large
lexicon around such topics as violence and drug-dealing, as well as
controversial or taboo subjects like sex, along with a range of other facets of
daily life[14]. This allows for a level of secrecy from controlling institutions,
especially the police, who are perceived as strongly biased against Beurs and
immigrants – the incident which sparked the recent riots of November 2005 was
the death of two young Beurs while hiding from (alleged) pursuit by the
authorities.   This was far from an isolated incident, and many see it as
systematic discrimination[15]. The importance of disguising words in Verlan can
be seen in the phenomenon of 'Reverlanisation' (or 'Veul'). This happens when
a word of Verlan becomes part of common parlance, and thus loses its 'edge'; in
an attempt to retain this, the process of Verlanisation is enacted again on the
already Verlanised word. Thus Beur becomes *Roeb* or *Reubeu*[16], one of the
latter being preferred to Beur, which is seen as having been co-opted into the
mainstream, and thus no longer belongs to the Beurs.

Shelta's relation to secrecy has become more controversial in recent
times. While it had long been accepted that altered Irish words formed much of
the lexicon of Shelta (Croften first noted this in the 1880s)[17], this has been
challenged as inaccurate, and contributing to negative stereotypes around
Travellers and crime, by implying that they have something to hide. This is a
live point of debate among Travellers (as well as in academia). While I see the
merits of the latter argument that places Shelta as a very old and independent
(insofar as any language can be), it is extremely difficult to substantiate.
Therefore, I have chosen to limit this study to Shelta in the modern period; that
is, the last 150 years or so. In this context, it is indisputable that the language
has served, in one of its major functions, as a tongue in which to disguise one's
meaning from an often hostile dominant sphere. This has been far from its only
function, as will be explored later, but the repeated testimony of Travellers such
as Pecker Dunne, that Shelta functions to help keep Travellers lives private and
for secrecy, can leave us in little doubt that disguising is (and has been for some
time) a very important part of Shelta use in the course of daily life[18]. Many of
the contexts in which secrecy in required, such as in business dealings with the

---

[13]Hargreaves, 'Resistance and Identity', p.94.

[14] Lefkowitz, '*Verlan*', p.317.

[15] Smith 'Playing with Fire'

[16] Lefkowitz, '*Verlan*', p.319.

[17] Ó hAodha, 'Travellers' Language', p.47.

[18] Pecker Dunne and Míchéal Ó hAodha *Parley-Poet and Chanter: Pecker Dunne an
autobiography* (Dublin, 2004), pp.52-53.

settled population, show the largest amount of innovation and alteration of any of the lexicon, i.e. *airgead* (money) has become *garead* or *goréad*, and more recently, *grade*. This has strong echoes of Verlan's alterations to keep ahead of common parlance. The involvement in crime of a small number of Travellers, and the generalised criminalisation of nomadism, mean that the vocabulary for police is also quite rich, another shared feature with the French language game. *Séideog* (one who blows, or gives out) has morphed into *séid* or *shade*[19], among other modifications, to keep ahead of the authorities[i].

The scale of usage in daily life is an important consideration in differentiating between the contexts and fashions in which Shelta and Verlan are used, and their importance therein. Shelta is felt very much as an important part of their heritage by Travellers, a historical bond exists[20]. And while there has undoubtedly been a resurgence in interest in the language in recent years, most accept that it is still under threat from disinterest in it, due to its association with more 'backward' times. This leads to a consciousness among its supporters, that Shelta is a cultural artefact with a value of its own, and this worth working to preserve. And while it is also used in many situations without thought of its political importance, this often forms a significant facet of Shelta's use – as part of Traveller's political project for proper recognition.

The 'cultural project' idea has interacted differently with the use of Verlan in France. As with Shelta, Verlan as a cultural marker/artefact is very much a concern of younger people forming an identity for themselves in which they can feel proud. The emergence of Verlan among Beurs in relatively recent times has had an explicitly subversive edge, and while initiatives like the famous 'Radio Beur' of the 1980s have sprung up, Verlan (and its speakers) have resisted codification, as explored earlier, in the form of rapid innovation and change[21]. This is an important differentiation between the two, for while both gain legitimacy from their relevance and identity function to the community, the political project of seeking recognition as an ethnic group means that many Travellers advance Shelta for acceptance by dominant society, for example in education[22]. The focus and coherence of this political project is not replicated by speakers of Verlan – nor do they seek to do so.

This divergence manifests itself in the present development of both Shelta and Verlan. These changes also undoubtedly represent, to a degree, reactions to the possibilities and limitations imposed by the place of Travellers

---

[19] Ó hAodha, 'Travellers' Language', p.56.
[20] Dunne and Ó hAodha, 'Parley-Poet and Chanter'.
[21] Hargreaves, 'Resistance and Identity', p.88.
[22] Alice Binchy, 'Shelta/Gammon in Dublin' in Acton, T.A. and Dalphinis, Morgan (eds.) *Language, Blacks and Gypsies: languages without a written tradition and their role in education* (London, 2000).

and Beurs occupy in wider society. As a very limited group, in terms of
numbers, in Irish society, and one whom many see as being under pressure from
the changes wrought by 'modernisation', the response of preservation and
inculcation of a new pride in culture is very understandable. That is not to say
that Shelta is stagnant, rather, it is a method of advocating their legitimacy. On
the other hand, the paradigm within which Verlan finds itself is more
consciously unmoved by the attitudes of dominant society and as such, this
fosters constant innovation to avoid comprehension by often oppressive forces
such as the police on the one hand, and co-option by (even sympathetic)
'outsiders' into common parlance, on the other[23]. In many ways, this dynamism
and constant change acts as a metaphorical two-fingers to the social mores of
what is seen as stuffy, old-fashioned and controlling French institutions and
customs.

Forging new identities of belonging

These linguistic revivals have formed important parts of building new group
identities for Travellers and Beurs to be a part of, and to feel pride in. This final
section will seek to examine the intertwining of language with belonging, in
order to further unpackage the commonalities that Shelta and Verlan share –
they are far from solely cryptic. In tandem with their use for secrecy, Shelta and
Verlan have also functioned to demarcate boundaries between different ethnic
groups, and thus build a sense of group solidarity, and also something of an 'us
against the world' siege mentality. The 'integrative function' of Shelta (for the
in-group) is emphasised by Binchy, allowing private expression of feelings
along with an idea of belonging which maintains the integrity of community
against 'incursions from the settled world'[24]. In a later work she also subsumes
the importance of disguise into this idea of a 'sacred' or unique and separate
language, refuting allegations of secrecy[25]. I feel that these are centrally
important to the use of Shelta, but disagree that secrecy is tangential – they must
both be accorded their place, as explored earlier: 'The existence of 'disguise'
processes in Shelta actually reflects the richness and antiquity of Shelta rather
than the opposite'[26].
The ability to appropriate words which Shelta has exhibited, and the dexterity
involved, stresses the breadth and scope of the language, and if much of this

---

[23] Lefkowitz, 'Verlan'.
[24] Binchy, 'Travellers' Language', p.147.
[25] Binchy, 'Shelta/Gammon in Dublin', p.130
[26] Ó hAodha, 'Travellers' Language', p.57.

comes from the contexts of criminalisation which Travellers face, little is served by attempts to deny this fact.

As touched upon earlier, the integrative function of both Shelta and Verlan in building a sense of belonging and group solidarity within the in-group is difficult to over emphasise. Shelta is seen as central to intergroup identity, as a marker of membership of the ethnic group [27]. This is an important battleground for Travellers, who are recognised as an ethnic group in the UK, but not in the Republic of Ireland[28]. It is widely accepted in linguistics that the acceptance of a group and that of their language are intimately intertwined. As such, the denigration of Travellers follows through onto their speech. Binchy examines how this fosters an 'us-against-the-world' mentality, which in turn builds a bond of acceptance by Travellers. This functions to integrate the community, in the maintence of the boundaries which mark belonging to the group[29]. And while this group may be ascribed low status by outsiders, this can be countered by a strong and positive self-perception within– this is intimately bound-up with language[30].

Much of this resonates clearly with the experience of Beurs and the adhesive quality that language brings to community. In France, Verlan has served to differentiate the Beurs both from mainstream French society and from their historical background, of which they also fell little ownership. Instead the Beurs search for their own cultural identity in which to invest value – a hybrid identity which takes account of the past, but which is not ruled by it[31]. As with Travellers and their speech, this is often rejected by others – so this rejection is turned into an affirmation of group integration and consciousness; "In a country obsessed with linguistic purity, it turns a stigma into a positive emblem, a form of covert prestige"[32]. Through its process of changing words, Verlan also adjusts their meaning, expressing positive attributes for the in-group, where mainstream society sees only problems. For example, in changing 'cité' to 'téci', words which nominally mean the same thing, but which change in implication from 'suburban dump for social outcasts' to 'homeland of the proud

---

[27] Ó Baoill, 'Travellers' Cant'
[28] Angelique Christafis 'Ireland's nomads expose a racial divide' *The Guardian* [online] November 25, 2005, http://www.guardian.co.uk/international/story/0,,1651134,00.html (14 April 2006).
[29] Binchy, 'Travellers' Language', p.147.
[30] Northover, quoted in Binchy, 'Travellers' Language', p.141.
[31] Nada Elia 'In the making: Beur fiction and identity construction', *World Literature Today*, 71 (1997), p.51.
[32] Lefkowitz, quoted in Alexander Stille 'Backward Runs French. Reels the Mind' *New York Times* [online]. http://www.mtholyoke.edu/~cskarocz/french370/boumkoeur/verlan.html (10 April 2006).

Beurs'[33]. This creates a strongly bonded group identity, providing a sense of belonging to those who often lack it.

The group identity of Beurs is also very much bound-up in the linguistics of Verlan. A generation of hip-hop artists were the first to unveil the depths of rage which permeated the peripheral (physically, socially and economically) Beurs[34], and in order to articulate their halfway-house between being French and being an immigrant, they turned to their own form of metaphorical 'talking back to authority'[35] – they turned to Verlan:

> A language of alienation that has, paradoxically, also become a means of integration, Verlan expresses France's love-hate relationship with its immigrant community[36].

Verlan has served as a rallying point for an explicitly anti-mainstream affirmation of group consciousness, which seeks to invert the negativity around Beurs, and create a sense of belonging to a different identity, which does not subscribe to the values to the French *jourbeois (bourgeois)* or those of their Muslim parents – they are hybrids[37]. The manner in which meanings are subverted and made positive, while insults become more powerful, is another notable feature of Verlan. Verlan allows for better expression of identity, and is jealously guarded by continued linguistic dexterity (such as the Reverlanisation examined earlier) from its attempted co-option by others[38]. Their method is different, but the desire for privacy and belonging within the group experience which this evidences is notable for its similarity to Shelta. This revival and creativity in Verlan also echoes Shelta in acting as a cultural marker of which to be proud, and as an important tool in fashioning group loyalty.

The inversion techniques that Shelta and Verlan share were what first drew attention to the potential for comparison. This work has tried to show that these similarities go much deeper than the surface. While it requires work of a greater scope to fully tease these out, we have seen the many commonalities of syntax alongside the similarities of origin in subordinated groups relegated to the periphery of the dominant society. There are also undoubted parallels between the solidarity drawn from language by the two groups in the course of fashioning a discourse of self-worth for their respective communities. There are

---

[33] Stille, 'Backward Runs French'.
[34] Mary Papenfuss 'French youths speaking their own language' *USA Today* [online] 5 January 2006. http://www.usatoday.com/news/world/2006-01-05-french-slang_x.htm (10 April 2006).
[35] Lefkowitz, *'Verlan'*, p.318.
[36] Stille, 'Backward Runs French'.
[37] Elia 'In the making',, p.50.
[38] Stille 'Backward Runs French'

obviously many dissimilarities between Shelta and Verlan, but the list of correspondence is impressive enough to pose many questions around the nature of subordination and responses to it, and the importance of language as a fluid entity and a tool of alienation, but also of integration.

References

Binchy, Alice, 'Shelta/Gammon in Dublin' in Acton, T.A. and Dalphinis, Morgan (eds.) *Language, Blacks and Gypsies: languages without a written tradition and their role in education* (London, 2000), pp.128-33.

Binchy, Alice, 'Traveller's Language: A Sociolinguistic Perspective' in McCann, May, Ó Síocháin, Séamus and Ruane, Joseph (eds.), *Irish Travellers: Culture and Ethnicity* (Belfast, 1994), pp.134-54.

—. 'Travellers' use of Shelta' in Kirk, John M. and Ó Baoill, Dónall P. (eds.), *Travellers and their Language* (Belfast, 2002), pp.11-19.

Christafis, Angelique, 'Ireland's nomads expose a racial divide' *The Guardian* [online] 26 November 2005. http://www.guardian.co.uk/international/story/0,,1651134,00.html (14 April 2006).

Dunne, Pecker and Ó hAodha, Mícháel, *Parley-Poet and Chanter: Pecker Dunne an autobiography* (Dublin, 2004).

Elia, Nada, 'In the making: Beur fiction and identity construction', *World Literature Today*, 71 (1997), pp.47-54.

Guene, Fazia, 'Back to the Streets' *The Guardian* [online] 24 December 2005. http://books.guardian.co.uk/comment/story/0,,1673488,00.html (10 April 2006).

Hargreaves, Alec G., 'Resistance and Identity in Beur Narratives', *Modern Fiction Studies*, 35 (1989), pp.87-102.

Henly, John, 'Do you speak Verlan?' *The Guardian* [online] 27 March 2000. http://www.guardian.co.uk/Columnists/Column/0,,221894,00.html (10 April 2006).

—. 'Try to be on-line, but don't be a hamster' *The Guardian* [online] 4 January 2003. http://www.guardian.co.uk/france/story/0,,868543,00.html (11 April 2006).

Jaccomard, Hélene, 'French against French: The uneasy incorporation of Beurs into French society' *Mots Pluriels*, 1 (1997).

Jeffries, Stuart, 'Teen gangs terrorise chic Paris' *The Observer* [online] 4 February 2001. http://observer.guardian.co.uk/international/story/0,,433307,00.html (11 April 2006).

Kirk, John M. and Ó Baoill, Dónall P. (eds.), *Travellers and their Language* (Belfast, 2002).

Lefkowitz, Natalie J., '*Verlan*: Talking backwards in French', *French Review*, 63 (1989), pp.312-22.

Macalister, R.A. Stewart, *The secret languages of Ireland: with special reference to the origin and nature of the Shelta language* (Cambridge, 1937).

McVeigh, Robbie, 'Theorising sedentarism' in Acton, T.A (ed.), *Gypsy Politics and Traveller Identity* (Hatfield, England: 1997), pp.1-26.

Ní Shuinéar, Sinead, 'The Curious Case of Shelta' Kirk, John M. and Ó Baoill, Dónall P. (eds.), *Travellers and their Language* (Belfast, 2002), pp.32-40.

—. 'Why do Gaujos hate Gypsies?' in Acton, T.A (ed.), *Gypsy Politics and Traveller Identity* (Hatfield, England: 1997), pp.27-54.

Ó hAodha, Mícháel, 'Travellers' Language: Some Irish Language perspectives' in Kirk, John M. and Ó Baoill, Dónall P. (eds.), *Travellers and their Language* (Belfast, 2002), pp.47-62.

Ó Baoill, Dónall P., 'Travellers' Cant – Language or Register' in McCann, May, Ó Síocháin, Séamus and Ruane, Joseph (eds.), *Irish Travellers: Culture and Ethnicity* (Belfast, 1994), pp.155-69.

Orlando, Valerie, 'From Rap to Rai in the mixing bowl: Beur hip-hop culture and banlieue cinema in urban France' *Journal of Popular Culture*, 36 (2003), pp395-415.

Papenfuss, Mary, 'French youths speaking their own language' *USA Today* [online] 5 January 2006. http://www.usatoday.com/news/world/2006-01-05-french-slang_x.htm (10 April 2006).

Poirier, Agnes, 'More liberty and equality' *The Guardian* [online] 9 November 2005. http://www.guardian.co.uk/comment/story/0,,1637161,00.html (9 April 2006).

Smith, Alex Duval, 'Playing with Fire' *The Observer* [online] 5 February 2006. http://www.guardian.co.uk/france/story/0,,1702321,00.html (9 April 2006).

Stille, Alexander, 'Backward Runs French. Reels the Mind' *New York Times* [online]. http://www.mtholyoke.edu/~cskarocz/french370/boumkoeur/verlan.html (10 April 2006).

Turner, Royce, 'Fellow Travellers' *The Guardian* [online] 24 August 1999. http://www.guardian.co.uk/comment/story/0,,266580,00.html (14 April 2006).

---

[i] It is important to note that this is not an attempt to further marginalise Travellers and Beurs by associating them with crime, rather to acknowledge that criminalisation is the reality of parts of **all** sidelined groups, and this need for secrecy has, in fact, lead to real creativity and invention.

CONTRIBUTORS

Thomas Acton is Professor of Romani Studies at the School of Social Sciences, University of Greenwich, UK . He is the first person to hold a chair in Romani Studies at any university and has always believed in the practical contribution scholarship can make to providing equality of opportunity and treatment for the Roma. Amongst his publications are:

Acton T. (1970) *Mo Romano Lil*; Oxford; Romanestan Publications

Acton T. (1981) *Gypsies;* Macdonald Education, London & Silver Burdett, New York

Acton T. and Gallant D. (1997) *Romanichals - the English Gypsies* Brighton: Wayland

Acton, T. (ed.) (1997) *Gypsy Politics and Traveller Identity*; Herts: University of Hertfordshire Press

Acton. T. and Mundy, G. (eds.) (1997): *Romani Culture and Gypsy Identity*; Herts: University of Hertfordshire Press.

Acton, T. (ed.) (2000) *Scholarship and the Gypsy Struggle*; Herts: University of Hertfordshire Press

Acton T. and Kenrick D.S (eds.) (1984) *Romani Rokkeripen To-Divvus: the English Romani dialect and its contemporary social, educational and linguistic standing;* London: Romanestan Publications

Jake Bowers is Britain's only Romani journalist. He is a regular contributor to the *Guardian, Independent, BBC Radio and Television, the Big Issue, Travellers Times* and the *Ecologist* on environmental and minority rights issues. He is also a founder of the *Gypsy Media Company*, Britain's only media company run by and for Gypsies themselves. The Gypsy Media Company specialises in communication, research and training projects about Britain's 300,000 Gypsies and Travellers.

Mary Burke is an Assistant Professor in the Department of English, University of Connecticut. Her research interests include Irish Literature (J.M. Synge, the Anglo-Irish Revival, Irish Minority Identities), Drama (The Abbey Theatre)

Anthony Drummond is a graduate of Social Policy. He is currently a third-year doctoral student at the University of Ulster where he is researching the experiences and the perceptions of Irish Travellers as relating to criminal justice on the island of Ireland, (North and South). In Ulster, he has worked as a voluntary Independent Representative for NIACRO. Prior to coming to Ulster he was employed as a Field Officer for English and Irish Travellers on an action research project funded by the Home Office, delivered by Bedfordshire Rural Communities Charity. Previous to that experience, he was employed as an assistant researcher at St. Mary's University College Twickenham on: *Room to Roam: England's Irish Travellers:* (http://www.irish.org.uk/research_roam.shtml).

Professor Ian Hancock, is Professor of Romany Studies at the University of Texas at Austin and is a renowned voice in the international Romany movement. He helped petition the United Nations in 1978 for membership of the International Romani Union and in UNICEF in 1987. He is an expert on the Romani Holocaust and served as a member of the U.S. Holocaust Memorial Council under President Clinton. On several occasions, he addressed the Organization for Security and Cooperation in Europe (OSCE) on Roma issues and collaborated with members of Congress on human rights projects. He is the recipient of the Norwegian Rafto Human Rights Prize and the Peace Award of the Bahá'í Church for his efforts to assist the Romani people. He has published a number of articles and books on Roma, including *We Are the Romani People: Ame Sam e Rromane Džene* (The University of Hertfordshire Press,2002), *The Pariah Syndrome: An Account of Gypsy Persecution and Slavery* (Karoma: Ann Arbor, 1987), and *A Handbook of Vlax Romani* (Slavica: Columbus, 1995).

Dr. Michael Hayes teaches in the Departments of English and History and Social Studies, University of Limerick on a number of modules relating to Traveller, Roma and Irish Migration. He has published a number of books about the ethnography and oral literature of a number of different cultural groups within the (traditionally nomadic) Irish Travelling community including: *Parley-Poet and Chanter* (2004); *The Candlelight Painter* (2004); *Canting with Cauley* (2005); *A Compendium of Fairground Speech* (2005); *Counter-Hegemony and the Irish "Other* (2006). *Irish Travellers: Representations and Realities* (2006)

Louise Harrington is a Development Worker with the Cork Traveller Women's Network (CTWN). Her book *Ireland's Forgotten "Others": Traveller Women and their Struggle for Cultural Recognition* is due to be published in 2007.

St. John Ó Donnabháin is a native of County Kilkenny and studied History, Politics and Sociology at the University of Limerick. His research interests include social inequality, gender and New Social Movements.

David O'Donnell is a researcher in the Intellectual Capital Research Institiute of Ireland, Limerick. After twenty years as a practitioner David re-discovered the Frankfurt School critical theory and research, particularly the recent work of Jürgen Habermas. His main research field is Intellectual Capital, hence the Intellectual Capital Research Institute of Ireland, with subsidiary interests in e-Democracy and critical management studies. He has published widely in journals such as the Journal of Intellectual Capital; the Journal of Information; Technology, Knowledge & Process Management; Human Resource Costing and Accounting; Cross-Cultural Management; International Journal of Manpower, International; MIT eCommerce Forum, book chapters, co-edited books and numerous conference presentations. He has a particular interest in applying insights from the Frankfurt School in collaborative, interdisciplinary work.

Dr Colm Power is Senior Postdoctoral Research Fellow in Criminal Justice and Ethnicity in the Centre for Ethnicity and Health, at the University of Central Lancashire. He wrote the Community Fund bid that gained £204,000 for a major social research project on Irish Travellers in England and was Principal Researcher on the project from 2000 to 2004. He is the author of both *Room to Roam: England's Irish Travellers* (Community Fund, London 2004); and *Are You Wide Pavee? An information booklet for Travellers* (Community Fund, London 2004).

Dr Joanna Richardson is a Senior Lecturer in the Department of Public Policy at De Montfort University. She teaches on undergraduate and postgraduate housing courses and has a research focus on Gypsies and Travellers, and how they are treated in society. Her book *The Gypsy Debate: Can Discourse Control?* was published in 2006 by Imprint Academic, Exeter. Joanna is currently working on a project for the Joseph Rowntree Foundation as relating to the issues of conflict resolution and new site provision as for Gypsies and Travellers. This report is due to be published in the summer of 2007.